Political
Pathfinders
L.B.T.H
1982-2017

MAYAR AKASH

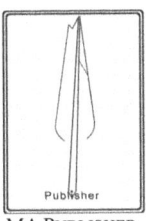

MA PUBLISHER

Political Pathfinders

Compiled & Written by Mayar Akash
Copyright © Mayar Akash 2022

Published by MA Publishing (Penzance)

ISBN-13:978-1-910499-31-3

All rights reserved. No part of this publication may be reproduced, stored in a retrieval system, or transmitted, in any form or by any means, electronic, mechanical, photocopying, recording, public performances or otherwise, without prior written permission of the copyright holder, except for brief quotations embodied in critical articles or reviews.

Forewards by Rajon Uddin Jalal
Copyedited by Abu Maryam Gous Ali
Cover designed by Mayar Akash
Typeset in Times Roman

Paper printed on is FSC Certified, lead free, acid free, buffered paper made from wood-based pulp. Our paper meets the ISO 9706 standard for permanent paper. As such, paper will last several hundred years when stored.

Acknowledgement

I would like to thank a number of people who have given me insight into the politics of Tower Hamlets.

Abdul Mukit Chunu MBE, Jainal Abedin, Helal Uddin Abbas, Shabina Aktar, Syed Mizan, Rajon Uddin Jalal, Ayas Miah, Shahid Ali and Mohammed Ali Nanu.

I would also like to acknowledge the following web site: www.lovewapping.org and Mark Baynes and www.trailbyjeory.com and trialby Jeory for their coverage. Both of these sites and the persons behind them have created an invaluable chronicle of the politics that takes place in Tower Hamlet and in particular their account of the Bangladeshi councillors.

Foreword

I am very pleased to write this forward for Mayar Akash and his new publication "Bangladeshi Political Pathfinders".

I have known Mayar Akash for around 35 years, we were both former residents of Tower Hamlets in London. We got to know each other through our community engagement, empowerment and development activities. His older brother Muhammad Ali was also a fellow Councillor with me at the London Borough of TowerHamlets.

Mayar Akash takes us through the journey of a very denigrated, deprived and disadvantaged Bangladeshi community in the East End of London, often ignored, neglected and forgotten by the relevant public and private authorities, institutions and establishments.

He also touches upon the racial tensions prevailing in East London throughout the 1970s and 1980s and how the community and anti-racist forces came together to defeat the racist thugs of the then National Front (NF) [an officially recognised political party], through the "Battle of Brick Lane in 1978". Many of the no-go areas for Bangladeshis of Tower Hamlets were made NF free zones through community campaigns and activism. The unity platform campaign slogans by the Bangladeshi youth and anti-racists included the following: **"here to stay here to fight;" "self-defence is no offence;" "end police brutality now;" "we demand equal rights" and "black and white unite and fight" etc.** These widely used and publicised slogans helped to express the public sentiments held by the decent multi-cultural & anti-racist communities of the time in East London, enabling us to mobilise people and community power against racism and fascism.

Racial attacks, harassment and even murders of Bengali/Asian and Black people on the streets of London were a daily and common phenomenon. The community responded vigorously following the murders of Altab Ali and Ishaque Ali in Tower Hamlets, Michael Ferreira in Hackney, Kenneth Singh in Newham, burning to death of the Khan family in Waltham Forest and Blair Peach [a teacher from Tower Hamlets] at a demonstration in Southall. The anti-racists and local community had concluded by then, **"enough is enough" and "the racist forces had to be defeated decisively"**. The Hackney and Tower Hamlets Defence Committee was established, like other anti-racist campaigns throughout the UK, to campaign against racism and fascism, **which eventually led to the NF being forced by people power, to relocating their**

Head Office from Hoxton [Bethnal Green to Welling [Kent] - on 16th October 1993!

Doors of the mainstream political parties were closed to the Bangladeshi and many other ethnic minority communities in Tower Hamlets and in other parts of the country. Once again, the community decided to takematters into their own hands and sponsored an independent political party called the "People's Alliance of East London" in 1982, which defeated the Labour incumbent in the Spitalfields Ward, sending shock waves throughout the Labour Party. This was because Labour was the only political party that enjoyed total political control of the borough. Successful election of the lone independent Councillor - Nurul Haque, forced the Labour Party to re-think their political strategy. In later years Bengalis made more political gains through the Labour Party, until the establishment decided that Bengali's participation should be **limited to Councillorships only**!

The white Working class people from the Isle of Dogs in Tower Hamlets laterresponded to the success of Bengali political advancement by electing their own BNP Councillor- Derek Beackon in the Millwall Ward (by-election, 1993). He was defeated one year later by the anti-racists.

The mainstream media, which had in reality ignored the existence of the large Bangladeshi and ethnic minority communities in East London, were forced to highlight their struggles after the success of the campaigns and mobilisations by the local community and anti-racist allies. This is when the entire United Kingdom became aware of the presence of the Bangladeshi community and their plight, needs and aspirations were widely reported through the mainstream media. Subsequently, the establishments were forced to take an interest in the more angry and boisterous Bangladeshi community.

The "Home Affairs Select Committee Report on Bangladeshis" published on 10th December 1986, created the appropriate momentum for challenging institutionalised racism and the doors of the mainstream public service providers begun opening up. The Bengalis were now beginning to access local authority public services like housing, social care and gaining grant awards for social, community and cultural projects. They were also getting recognition and representation through organisations like the former Greater London Council and inner London Education Authority [both led by Ken Livingstone]. Indeed, there were discussions about the Bangladeshi community in the House of Commons. The Bangladeshi community of Britain was now placed firmly on the mainstream political agenda.

However, institutionalised racism within the mainstream political parties once again showed its ugly face and those who had made progress through participation in mainstream political parties and institutions, had to leave their chosen political parties and form their own independent platforms to partially and successfully challenge the betrayal of mainstream political parties and the establishments. The reactionary and right wing elements within the Labour Party wanted to ensure that the Bengali candidates did not make it above Councillorship and that is why parachuted in Oona King and made her an MP for Bethnal Green and Bow in 1997. The declaration of an illegal war on Iraq by Tony Blair galvanised community resistance and a new wave of politics so the arrival of the RESPECT Party [George Galloway, who replaced Oona King when in 2005], Tower Hamlets First [Lutfur Rahman] and People's Alliance of Tower Hamlets-PATH [Rabina Khan]. The latter two of the newly formed local political parties were eventually defeated by the mainstream media, political establishments and the British Judiciary. The later occurrence of disunity amongst the independents themselves, primarily based on personalities, positions and status resulted in the public losing confidence in the newly founded political platforms and eventually led to victory for the right wing reactionaries!

Although, at the moment we have two Labour Bengali female MPS from Tower Hamlets [Rushanara Ali (2010) andApsana Begum (2019)] and four altogether in London [including Tulip Siddiq (2015) and Rupa Huq (2015)], but the political machinery is still controlled by our old masters and they are not interested in allowing the Bengalis to make any further progress! Bengalis are one of the most politically active communities in the UK, yet the Mayor of Tower Hamlets, which is the heart of the Bangladeshi community, is a right wing and bigoted white politician! Equally it is sad to note that the Bengali MPs do not have the prospect of joining the Shadow Cabinet or gain Ministerial jobs in the near future [because the reactionary and right wing Tory party is in power]!

I hope that many more people from the younger generations of the Bangladeshi community like Mayar Akash will record the historical inspirations, failures and achievements of our communities, so that we have a widespread record of community history for the future generations to benefit from.

Rajonuddin Jalal
17th August 2020
Chairperson-East London Community Trust-ELCT [UK]
An Advisor-Altab Ali Foundation-AAF [UK]

Contents

Acknowledgement	3
Foreword	4
Contents	7
Introduction	9
Visionary	14
Placid Community Under Threat	16
British National Party In Our Community	16
Community's Resolve	21
Earliest Political Pioneers	30
The Break Through	31
1982's	33
St Katharine's Ward	52
Bangladeshi Women	56
Millwall	58
Respect Party	59
Conservative	66
Labour Party Glory Days	67
Political Playing Field Is Changing	68
Party Forming	70
Rabina Khan's Road From Thing To Path	71
Party Hopping	74
Break Down Of The Votes	75
Allowances	78
Aptitude	80
Discontent	81
Bad Press	82
2010	85
Candidates Per Party	89
Councillors: Per Election	90
How Many Councillors By Ward	91
The First Councillors In Each Ward	94
Bangladesh Connection	97
Elected Male Councillors:	102
Elected Female Councillors:	108
Full List:	109
List Of All Bangladeshi Female Candidates	128
Tower Hamlet's Election Results	130
Community Progression	130
Full Election Results	133
1986-1990 Election	135

1990-1994 Election	138
1994-1998 Election	142
1998-2002 Election	146
2002-2006 Election	151
2006-2010 Election	160
2010-2014 Election	169
2014-2018 Election	178
LBTH Mayoral	188
Battle For Parliament	189
Abbreviations	192
Bibliography	193
References	194
MAPublisher Catalogue	195

Introduction

Pathfinder is a continuation from the "Tower Hamlets Bangladeshi Politicians' reference book 1982-2017". In this book you will find data which I did not include in the first book as I thought it will over-shadow the positivities that I aimed to highlight of the Bangladeshi community. I aim to present the fact and first-hand accounts for the current and future generations; in a way that is insightful and easy to digest, with pictures and brief notes/comments and tables.

Our community has progressed in leaps and bounds, so, plotting the community's journey, in particular from 1982 and dip into 1978 when the placid community decided to mobilise themselves from the strangle hold of the racism in all walks of life living in the East End of London.

We will also look at what the internal issues were, and how they were overcomed, challenged and changed. Why did it take so long for the community to mobilise itself?

It is important to notemap the transition of the Bangladeshi community in the United Kingdom, starting with Tower Hamlets, where many of the beginnings were but not exclusively.

Pathfinder looks at what the political parties did, and are doing to help the community; how many people they supported and map the growth. Look at how the community grew in local politics in strength and numbers, and the strategies used. To acknowledge all the people of Bangladeshi decent who put themselves forward to campaign and stand for election.

Pathfinder looks at and highlights the fascists who tried to get into politics as well as to give an actual insight to the numbers of racists living in the borough and see the changes in numbers. They made our lives a misery in our everyday life and their desire to get into local politics to further hurt us through policies and services, yet the resilience of my elders in the community grew as it overcame many obstacles, such as the "Paki bashing".

After the murder of Altab Ali in Whitechapel and the death of Ishaque Ali and Ambor Ali in 1978, the community found itself cornered in all levels, police, local authorities, councillors and that is it had to solidify its resolves as the killings put the people in survival mode. The community through various groups and agencies' support became proactive in fighting the racists out on the streets.

The vanguards knew that fighting on the streets alone will not suffice; they needed to get into the Town Hall. Reflecting back on the community's action, the new six year old community was fighting their 2nd war in England, the very people, Altab, Ishaque, Ambor Ali and thousands of other who paid for the liberation war for Bangladesh, was now paying with their lives in the United Kingdom, in the East End of London, the Spitalfields in particular; to liberate the community.

There have been a few momentous occasions for the Bangladeshi community living in East London, Tower Hamlets, England, United Kingdom.

1965   When Aftab Ali ensured for many East Pakistanis to be allowed to come to the UK on work voucher permits.

1970   Murder of Tosir Ali in Bromley, East London.

1972   When the news of the Independence broke the community would have rejoiced with their new identity, from East Pakistanis to Bangladeshis.

1978   The death of Altab Ali, one of the youths, when the youth of then changed the narratives of the Bangladeshi community. When reality was realised, the community is here to stay and not in perpetual sojourning.

1982   Election of two Bangladeshi councillors in Tower Hamlets

1985   Home Office Committee - Review of the Bangladeshi Community

> HOUSE OF COMMONS
>
> # HOME AFFAIRS COMMITTEE
>
> Race Relations and Immigration Sub-Committee
>
> Session 1985–86
>
> **BANGLADESHIS IN BRITAIN**
>
> MINUTES OF EVIDENCE
>
> Monday 24 March 1986
>
> **Department of the Environment**
>
> Sir George Young MP, Mr D R Lewis, Mrs J M Williams, Mr J G Grevatt and Mr M B M Harryman
>
> Ordered by The House of Commons to be printed
> 24 March 1986
>
> LONDON
> HER MAJESTY'S STATIONERY OFFICE
> £4.20 net

Images from the Tower Hamlets archive library

1990   When the first Bangladeshi woman councillor was elected, Mrs Pola Manzila Uddin.

HOUSE OF COMMONS

First Report from the

HOME AFFAIRS COMMITTEE

Session 1986–87

BANGLADESHIS IN BRITAIN

Volume I

Report together with the Proceedings of the Committee

*Ordered by The House of Commons to be printed
10 December 1986*

LONDON
HER MAJESTY'S STATIONERY OFFICE
£4.70 net

Images from the Tower Hamlets archive library

1998 - When Mrs Pola Manzila Uddin received her peerage to become the first Bangladeshi Baroness, who entered the House of Lords before anyone entering House of Commons, Parliament.

2010 - The election of Ms Rushanara Ali to becoming the first Bangladeshi MP, Member of Parliament.

2010 - Election of the First Statutory Mayor in Tower Hamlets, Mr Lutfur Rahman.

These are the moments when the community was catapulted to another level in the wider community and world standing.

This community has been and still is subjected to many different strains of effects from myriad of policies in the borough locally and nationally which changes the shape of our 'integration.' So, the focus is on the political development and growth of the community in the last 35 years, since 1982 to 2017.

There is so much to focus on and pick from, but this is a start in the recounting the scenes and settings of the past, so that they can be presented in the best way possible for the current and future generations to appreciate what they have and enjoy; and also to ensure that they will never return back to the past.

Visionary

There are many pioneers of the seventies through the Pakistani Welfare Association (PWA) to then in 1972 becoming the Bangladeshi Welfare Association (BWA) paved the way for this journey. While there are many, one particular person I was fortunate to share some working and professional time with, it was the late Mr Tassaduq Ahmed, he was devoted to the progression of the community, to the point where he volunteered his time to PWA, to be the secretary.

This was one of Mr Tassaduq Ahmed's initiatives to help and support the community.

He was one of the progressive and forward thinking vanguards of the community for many of us, he had a vision of the future where he saw his community integrating into Britain and the British identity. He worked towards bridging the gap in the processes of integration; he worked towards building better understanding and facilitating multiculturalism, enabling acceptance and tolerance to fit into the United Kingdom, fusing into the British way of living.

> **BRITISH BENGALIS IN SEARCH OF AN IDENTITY**
> by Tassaduq Ahmed
>
> The opening of the Nazrul Centre in Spitalfields is another landmark in the efforts of the Bengali-speaking British residents in their search for an identity for themselves within the framework of the multiracial and multicultural British society. It is therefore the hope of all that the centre would also be the nucleus of activities that would draw in the cream of the Bengali community and motivate them towards changing some of their attitudes and behaviour patterns so that unitedly they could try to lay a stable foundation of a truly multicultural community life in Spitalfields. And no other area is more suitable for such a pioneering work.
>
> For the British Bengalis Spitalfields - with its long history as a host to waves of persecuted and disadvantaged immigrants from different parts of Europe and lastly from the Asian subcontinent - is destined to play a leading role. It is in Spitalfields that leading organisations of the British Bengalis took their birth and were reared since 1953. It is here that we have seen the surfacing of young Bengalis as a powerful social force in 1978 as a protest movement against the racist murder of Aftab Ali. That protest movement is trying to consolidate its achievement through the creation of the Nazrul Centre. What Spitalfields is trying to do today will inevitably be followed up by British Bengalis elsewhere. This is the lesson we are to draw from what has been happening over the last three decades and when planning for the future this perspectives should never be lost sight of.
>
> The first major effort to inspire the British Bengalis with the urge to seek their identity and to give them a sense of history was undertaken in 1962. Professor Nazmul Karim, late Dr Alim Chaudhury and late Shawkat Ali were instrumental in setting up the London Bangla Academy at 24 Great Windmill Street, Piccadilly circus, London W.1. The Academy was accomodated in a small room placed at the disposal of the institute by late Ali. This room housed a small library and was the meeting place of the Academy for the next few years. The main aim then was to set up a small library and a reading room for Bengalis in and around London. Professor Karim also used to guide a study group on Bengali arts and literature. Later some of the activists of this Study group decided to set up a permanent centre. The idea consolidated into a project to buy a freehold premises. As a result the East Pakistan House was born with its own premises at 91 Highbury Hill, Finsbury, London N.5. It also served as a hostel for Bengali community workers most of whom at a later period became activists in support of the Bengaldesh movement. The Bengali monthly journal styled 'PURBA BANGLA' became the mouthpiece of this group and this journal played an important role in the campaign to build up support for the needs and demands of the then East Pakistan (now Bangladesh). Subsequently during 1970/71 the East Pakistan House fell into disrepair and after the departure of the then literary secretary Sukumar Mazumdar the Bengla Academy became defunct.
>
> Since then there has been a substantial growth of Bengali population in the UK and an increased awareness of the importance of mother tongue teaching. In the course of the last decade community workers from both Bengals have increasingly involved themselves in mother tongue teaching in Bengali. Most of these institutions have been built by voluntary efforts. As a result a need arose to exchange experiences in this field. In response to this demand the London Bangla Academy was revived. The first effort to revitalise the Bangla Academy was undertaken in 1980 after the very successful mounting of the Arts of Bengal Exhibition at the Whitechapel Art Gallery in 1979. Subsequently two formal meetings of the sponsors were held and the London Bangla Academy was reconstituted in its present structure with the primary aim to give support to the teaching of Bengali as mother tongue and as second language to foreigners. It is now headed by three co-presidents, namely Lulu Bilquis Banno, Ketaki Kushari Dyson and William Radice. The Academy is also committed to give back-up support to the Kobi Nazrul Centre. If the blending between the academics and grassroot movement could be properly forged that would open up possibilities for a new future.

This is an example of his written records of his vision for the community; however, the British Bangladeshi community had mountains to climb then.

15

Placid Community Under Threat

British National Party in our community

From the murder of Tosir Ali in 1970, and the Bangladesh independence onwards and after the murder of Altab Ali in 1978 by the racists, bigots in the face of the Bangladeshi community were a constant fear and danger in the lives of the people for many years. They have reared their ugly heads and tormented the community indiscriminately. They have canvassed their candidates throughout the eighties, nineties and twenties.

1978 saw the true Britishness of the Bangladeshi youths, Altab Ali's peers and friends were integrating into the British way of living from the grass root level. They were the youth that came over from Bangladesh, uprooted to face the challenges of the nation at the time with mass unemployment, coupled with a foreign language with the harsheties of the less educated low skilled 'indigenous' East End white community. They began to root themselves in Britain, in the East End of London, Tower Hamlets, Spitalfields, St Katharine's and west sides of the borough. They were able to galvanise and channel their energy and lives as they hadn't yet established a family of their own,

The borough had pockets of NF/BNP in many wards like Millwall, Bow, Bromley-by-Bow, Langdon Park, Weavers and so on. I guess one thing is clear; you have to live in the wards to soak up the climate of the area. Having spoken to people from the Wapping area, where there was a constant racial tension, they were always on alert and the attacks were so frequent that they weren't shocked to hear about the attack on Quddus Ali, the boy who got attacked (1993) and was left for dead. This was their reality and they were de-sensitised and battle hardened.

To get a picture of the BNP/NF's involvement in the election you can see from the data collated in the table, how active they have been, and how many racist we have living in the borough and what wards.

While racism goes back decades, it is in the early 70s when the attacks on the Bangladeshi in the East End of London escalated. It is clear that the BNP/NF political activity wained from after 1982 elections when two Bangladeshi councillors won seats against the odds. Fortunately no National Front candidate won

The National Front (NF) & British National Party (BNP)

This is the table that lists all the National Front candidates who stood in the 1978 election in Tower Hamlets.

Ward	Election	Electors	T'out	Candidate	Party	Votes
Blackwall	1978	4,947	20.9	G.L. Davis	NF	108
Blackwall				Ms. B.J. Matthews	NF	97
Bow	1978	4,568	33.7	R. Cribb	NF	99
Bow				A.R. Buttery	NF	98
Bow				E.J. Bale	NF	88
Bromley	1978	6,166	27.3	K.M. Jones	NF	177
Bromley				S. Muzzlewhite	NF	149
Bromley				Ms. T.I. Rowe	NF	141
East India	1978	5,012	30.1	Ms. I.M. Berry	NF	191
East India				R. Underwood	NF	152
Grove	1978	4,451	39.5	E.J. Smith	NF	90
Grove				J.A. Buttery	NF	89
Holy Trinity	1978	6,819	25.8	Ms. I.R. Underwood	NF	254
Holy Trinity				M.G. Rowe	NF	230
Holy Trinity				G.A. Williams	NF	207
Lansbury	1978	6,295	27.4	S.D. Colville	NF	227
Lansbury				S.H. Buttery	NF	225
Lansbury				Mrs. M.A. Rowe	NF	199
Limehouse	1978	7,147	24	V.J. Clark	NF	221
Limehouse				J.W. Tear	NF	200
Limehouse				T.B. Rowe	NF	191
Millwall	1978	7,144	24.4	K.P. Griffin	NF	236
Millwall				P.J. Edwards	NF	224
Millwall				D. Williams	NF	170
Park	1978	4,638	38.6	T.J. Matthews	NF	128
Park				Mrs. R. Muzzlewhite	NF	122
Redcoat	1978	5,338	28.6	T.J. Godden	NF	144
Redcoat				Mrs. M.A. Matthews	NF	125
St Dunstan's	1978	6,698	27	R.J. Bargery	NF	200
St Dunstan's				Mrs. S. Bale	NF	163
ST Jame's	1978	4,922	26.6	P.J. Beresford	NF	233
ST Jame's				F.J. Nail	NF	228
St Katharine's	1978	6,166	27.8	J.W. Muzzlewhite	NF	108
St Mary's	1978	5,351	31.7	J.W. Gibbons	NF	56
St Mary's				T.J. Jellis	NF	52
St Peter's	1978	7,809	25.3	A. Mariner	NF	401
St Peter's				G.P. Newman	NF	376
Shadwell	1978	6,059	30.9	T. Underwood	NF	155
Spitalfields	1978	6,273	28.5	A.J. Bennett	NF	87
Weavers	1978	6,609	28.5	R. Newman	NF	216
Weavers				T.G. Courtney	NF	214
Weavers				B. Gilbert	NF	213
		112412	0		42	7284

This table paints a picture of the 'host' community of the borough that the Bangladeshi community were living amongst. This also gives an insight as to why the Paki Bashing was so prevalent and lasted for the period it did. The elders/voters influenced the members of their family - the impressionable 'lad'.

Ward	Voters	Ranked most racist ward
Blackwall	205	
Bow	285	
Bromley	467	
East India	343	
Grove	179	
Holy Trinity	691	2
Lansbury	651	3
Limehouse	621	6
Millwall	630	5
Park	250	
Redcoat	269	
St Dunstan's	363	
St James's	461	
St Katharine's	108	
St Mary's	108	
St Peter's	777	1
Shadwell	155	
Spitalfields	87	
Weavers	643	4

The table also indicates the ward with the most racist voters. It may not represent the level of racists in each ward based on votes. However it provides a picture of the process of integration into British way of life by the first and second generation in the East End.

The most racist wards based on the table above were as follows: who had over 600 votes. These wards dwarfed the other wards:

        1. St Peter's   777
        2. Holy Trinity 691
        3. Lansbury   651
        4. Weavers   643
        5. Millwall   630
        6. Limehouse 621

Bromley - 467 and St James - 461 votes were the middle clusters racist ward. Looking at this table gives us a "racist picture," demographics of the borough.

By NF/BNP standing for election was an attack in itself on the community and on a higher level, the strategy and tactics of the racists have moved from the street level "Paki Bashing" to "Paki Bashing Legitimisation," where it is at the policy making level. These tables are to illustrate to the community that there is no place for complacencies. It is the community's own diligence to ensure that BNP does not place itself in the heart of the Bangladeshi community ever again.

How times have changed and how the Bangladeshi community had to adapt, from the "Paki bashing" era of the 60s till the mid nineties, where people were attacked, mugged and killed until the community's mobilisation in groups after the death of Tosir Ali in 1970, then the elders mobilised themselves, such as the Pakistani Welfare Association (PWA) and after the liberation it became known as Bangladesh Welfare Association (BWA) from 1972 and who were part of the vanguards in 1978.

The youth of pre-78 era growing up under the protection of the BWA took on responsibilities and went on to challenge the status quo of the community elders. Many of whom went on to become the main body of the present councillorship (up till 2017). The youth of the 70s were lead by community champions that were from the educated, professional and legal background, such as Abdul Aziz who specialised in immigration law, Shaha Lutfur Rahman to name a couple, they mentored the likes of Abdul Mukit Chunu MBE, Rajon Uddin Jalal and many others. Through their support, the youth of the 70s got capacity building facilitation from various agencies including Avenues Unlimited, Toc H and others. They then went on to formed groups and mobilised themselves and other youth and defended the community via groups couple of names of these groups were the Bangladeshi Youth Front (BYF), Bangladeshi Youth Movement (BYM) and others.

So the racism on the doorsteps took decades to change, so then, the National Front took to focusing on the weekends where they would sell their news papers at the Brick Lane Sunday Market. There was always pressure put by the elders of the community on the authorities to address the issues of the fascist group. To some extent it was a successful campaign and the following outcomes came about; the National Front reduced their presence to a limited time slot, but then they re-branded themselves to British National Party (BNP).

The BNP were allowed to continue to sell the paper as part of preserving their freedom of speech, they were allowed to sell the newspaper on Sundays. This went on for many years until 1993, when they put a candidate up for local election; Mr Derek Beackon, who got elected in 1993.

Following table lists all the National Front and British National Party candidates that stood for election in Tower Hamlets after the 1978s election results.

Year	Ward	No	Votes	Name
1986	Holy Trinity	1	212	D Ettridge
1986	St Dunstan's	1	256	R.S Evans
1990	Redcoat	1	93	D.W. Beackon
1990	Spitalfields	1	70	K.A Walsh
1993	Millwall	1	1480	D.W. Beackon
1994	Holy Trinity	3	786	D.M. King
1994	Holy Trinity		743	Mrs L. Miller
1994	Holy Trinity		737	E. J. McHale
1994	St Peter's	1	889	P. Maxwell
1995	Spitalfields	1	82	K.A Walsh
1995	Weavers	1	486	D.M. King
1998	Holy trinity	1	147	P. Costello
1998	St James's	2	168	P. Maxwell
1998	St James's		168	P.E. McHale
2001	Holy Trinity	1	74	Mrs L. Miller
2002	Bethnal Green North	1	162	William Frederick Wren
2002	Millwall	1	204	Gordon Thomas Callow
2006	Mile End & Globe Town	3	411	Gordon Thomas Callow
2006	Mile End & Globe Town		375	William Frederick Wren
2006	Mile End & Globe Town		186	Jefrey Christopher Marshal
2008	Millwall	1	219	Jefrey Christopher Marshal
2008	Weavers	1	154	Russel Pick
2010	Bow East	1	318	Mike Underwood
2010	East India & Lansbury	1	400	John Searle
2010	Mile End & Globe Town	1	284	Russel Pick
2010	Millwall	1	358	Dave Anderson

The stoppage of their newspaper sale took place in the early part of 1990's when my generation took the position in time to respond, running up to the 1993 election. Quddus Ali was beaten so badly he was in a coma for four months. Several men and a woman were arrested but only one of the men was charged but later released.

Paki Bashing got stopped through the vigilante groups who went onto become community groups with structure, constitution and with mission statements.

In the late eighties new breeds of Bangladeshi youth prevail, the community's youth got into gang mentality and there were gang battles within the Bangladeshi youth in the borough, turf war, music groups, estate posses and in particular the Brick Lane Mafia. The "Pack" mentality prevailed and there the wolves and the tigers at large, there was no more getting away with "Paki Bashing," they now thought back, hammer, mechetes, knives, axes, iron bars and so on.

With this mind a group of youth set up on a Sunday demonstration day, on a rooftop in Bethnal Green where the newspaper seller stand and started throwing misiles down on them.

The Newspaper selling got stopped by the youth through demonstration and confrontation supported by external agency. Later the elected BNP candidate was ousted by the mums and dads taking to the street to ensure that every single Bangladeshi and all anti racist voters came out and voted, this was illustrated by the result of the general election in 1994.

Community's resolve

All community activities and attentions were rooted in Spitalfields, where they were taking the main challengers from the heartlands of the Sylheti community. Md Ashik Ali was a Labour party member and he had the full backing from the Labour party, however the community leaders were being undermined by Political parties; leaving the people of the heartland, Brick lane, Spitalfields and the surrounding area to fight.

Here is an extract from Faruque Ahmed's book "Bengal Politics in Britain, Logic, Dynamics and Disharmony," where he gives account of what had taken place running upto the 1982 election.

> *"Altab Ali's death was the turning point for the Bengali community to move forward. Muhammad Nurul Huque, Shirajul Haq, Golam Mostafa, Abdul Barik, Rafique Ullah, Shoaib Choudhury, Zia Uddin Lala, Dr Zaidul Hasan, Dr Haris Ali, Ashuk Miah, Abdul Kadir Miah, Azad Khan and others boldly challenged the local Labour Party. Throughout*

1981, Muhammad Nurul Huque and his colleagues were busy in organising an 'Alliance' consisting of different groups to stand in the 1982 council elections. As a result, as many as 20 Bengali community organisations got together under the auspice of the Bangladesh Welfare Association to ensure the participation of Bengali leaders in the elections. They convened the first meeting at the Montifiore Centre and their call for "Unity of the Community" won the day; the People's Democratic Alliance (PDA) was formed. After one week, another meeting was held at the Montefiore Centre. Subsequent meetings were held at the Toynbee Hall and Bangladesh Welfare Association office (39 Fournier Street, London E1). The PDA unanimously agreed to support the independent Bengali candidates against the Labour candidates. Altogether nine Bengali individuals offered their candidacy from the Spitalfields, St Katharine's, St Mary's and Weavers ward in that election. Spitalfields attracted the greatest competition, as five Bangladeshi (four independent and one SDP candidate). They are PDA nominated independent candidate Muhammad Nurul Huque and Syed Nurul Islam, SDP nominated candidate Golam Mustafa and other independent candidate was Shirajul Haq and Abdul Gofur (late Abdul Gofur Khalisader).
The fact that a Bengali candidate was able to win an election changed the approach of mainstream political parties to Bengali community forever."

The Chosen One

Md Nurul Huque was a Professor in History in Bangladesh and he had a good acumen and was selected by the elders of the community to stand for election in 1982. Many others also stood either with or without the support of the elders.

Md Nurul Huque was the people's choice of Spitalfields.

Md Nurul Huque - before coming to UK, in the late seventies and in 2017.

1st 3 Photos supplied by Md Nurul Huque, fourth one taken by Mayar Akash at his residence in London, UK.

There was discontent from the community leaders in Spitalfields area, Ashik Ali was viewed by the people in Spitalfields as the Labour party's candidate. Ashik Ali was a benefactor of the sentiments from the murder of Altab Ali, who lived in that ward and also lived in the same building on the council estate as Mr Ashik Ali.

Altab Ali was deprived of his democratic right to vote by his killers in 1978. It was fitting for the sentiment of Altab Ali to secure a Bangladeshi Labour seat in the area. The residents of Reardon house and the wider community worked hard to see it through to get a Bangladeshi councillor.

> *"That was a great achievement on his part to get elected*
> *In what was really a hostile political environment as an Independent.*
> *He must have found as a pioneer, very very difficult to operate as a councillor."*
>
> Interview with Phil Maxwell, Ex Councillor

While the blood of murdered Altab Ali leaves an imprint in 1978, his was not the only death, Ishaque Ali and Ambor Ali were also killed after him, within months that year; and as a result Mr Ashik Ali got a wider response and involvement from two boroughs. People from Tower Hamlets and Hackney got together and drove the anti-racist agenda forward and kept it alive. This momentum's, the inertia became relentless as there were demonstrations after demonstrations to ensure that the fascists were ousted and the people got the rights they were denied in all walks of life.

The Pathfinders

These two individuals became the beacon for the next set of councillors.

Majority of the Tower Hamlets activists forged places and positions in the community and for the first time the youth were on an even playing field with the elders of the community, mainly members of Bangladeshi Welfare Association BWA and others.

The death of Altab and the others had resonated and ensured that the community could not stay complacent and look to the authorities; like in the past when the community elders relied on the authorities, and didn't belive in taking direct action. The new energies of the young people were not going to tolerate it anymore, and there was news and words in the air to have their own councillor.

To have their own councillor whether the parties supported them or not; and there was no way of going back. This was the beginning of the new aged era in the Bangladeshi Politics. While there wasn't an overarching support for Mr Ashik Ali from the Brick Lane lot, their respective residents supported them in their own wards.

> *"Again, when one reflect on the spark or the impetus of this drive to get to the platform from where they can make active changes, it only leads to that one moment in time, 7.30pm 4th of May 1978, when the blood squirted out of Altab Ali's neck and the chest, and when and where through his actions; he said no, you are not going to stop me, I am going to make it to the bus stop where I will get help; I have made arrangement to vote today, my family is waiting for me at Reardon street.*
>
> *This is the moment, this, the vote; each Bangladeshi voter makes on Election Day, each year, everytime for always."*

While that was the resolve of the community as a whole, but for the Sylheti community, there were factions, steming from a rural, tribal/clan and class orientated background, very inwardly discriminitive. Many of the candidates had been scrutinised and this is a historical fact etched into individuals who pursued a career in the 1982 race. Many have failed since, due to inherent lack of support from the core, the grand mafias of the community, generally made up of educated and well-off individuals from 'back home' and people who have been successful in business here in the UK.

Community Selection criteria

Generally people "well off" from India/East Pakistan who came over here continued to do well and thus have automatically continued the hierarchical system from back home. The system is similar to the Hindu caste system, aristrocrats, land owners look down on the tradesmen of the country, such as fishermen, black smiths to farmers' etcetera. God forbid if you or your family had any blemishes such as divorce or a criminal record or even had married a white woman (whether English, Irish, Welsh, Scottish or European), or if you had been seen drinking or socialising in the pubs. All of this is frowned upon and enough to be ostracised for.

The above list is just a few, but many of those discriminating criterias still exist however, much has changed due to the integration and the effects permeating from that. The attitudes of each new generation have changed by half each time, it has come to a point in time that the community has moved into new realms, where new cultural identities have formed and many now don't inherently feel or associate themselves as being the old Bangladeshi.

We also have accounts noted by Sarah Glynn in her book "Class, Ethicity and Religion in the Bengali East End, A Political history from different key people describing how their experiences and actions will have influenced the elders' attitudes then.

Sarah Glynn notes Rajon Uddin Jalal's:

> *"The main inspiration behind the movement was Shah Lutfur Rahman, one of the leaders of the British section of the Bengali pro-Peking Left in 1971. The BYM was founded in 1976 and grew out of the evening classes Shah had been running for young Bengalis since the mid-60s, which often ended in the pub – a radical step itself."*

We also have a personal account from Suhail Aziz, in his book "Breakthrough memoir of a British-Trained Bangladeshi," where he gives accounts of his experience with the community and why he didn't get a political position:

> *"It must be said that some so-called leaders in my Sylheti community did not like my involvement in the East End – Brick Lane, Aldgate, Spitalfields, Bethnal Green and other pockets of Tower Hamlets where Bangladeshis lived and worked in relatively large numbers. They saw me as an 'immigrant from South London' who had no business to be there...*
>
> *But no doubt there was some jealousy and resentment towards me. Some even saw me as a 'treat,'*
>
> *...to be obstructed by the 'village politics of Brick Lane'."*

Community bias

So keeping to the time, Helal Uddin Abbas was one of the first Labour party members in the Sylheti community to enter into the local political arena. He was the new second generation youth of the time who went on to become the third councillor for the Bangladeshi community and the first Sylheti one, as Md Ashik Ali and Md Nurul Huque were not from Sylhet and thus did not subscribe to those minds, quirks of the villagers.

Therein the community lies an inherent dislike for non-Sylheti to take control over the Sylheti community. This emanates from back home as the Sylheti community is looked down upon by the non Sylhetis, from the other districts of Bangladesh. This is something we will explore in another book, but keeping that in mind, it is ironic that the Sylhetis chose the best candidate to put through for the election. This would have been a double edged decision by the elders as there were no suitable candidates in their opinion, who had the acumen it required for a councillor. However, there were other Sylhetis who went against the community elders and stood for election

The community needed to change the Labour party, its membership and representation.

The Bangladeshi people naturally homed in with the Labour party and stayed loyal until Tony Blair came in government and the Iraq war took place.

The community has come a long way in the last 35 years and has altered and shaped the current and evolving community. The benefits of the early councillors and changing the face of the borough and access to resources and services has empowered as well as corrupted.

It is clear from history that there were many people in the community from all walks of life. There were educated individuals amongst the not so educated village individuals and those that were naturally savvy thinkers.

The community had the Bangladesh Welfare Association with the likes of Late Tassaduk Ahmed and others who were educated and community activists, but for whatever reason they were not amongst those at the frontline or in the limelight.

The 1980s was a huge and significant period for the community and this would be likened to sending someone to space. The community had to select the best candidate who will be competent and representative of all, in terms of education, experience, professionalism and articulation.

The community went through myriad of issues and selection process, the classic community traits came out, the selection and de-selection was based on the cast and class system borne out of rural Bangladesh.

The community elders were critical in selecting the individual candidates; they would have gone through many screening processes, such as their family background, their profession 'back home', status 'back home' and here in the UK community.

This would have been tedious, punitive and backwards, this would have caused many quarrels, infighting and disunity. However, two candidates did get selected with the key decision making individual's backing. The two selected were Mohammed Ashik Ali who was a Labour party member, and Mohammed Nurul Huque who was a paid member, but due to misunderstandings relating to the annual fees, he didn't know he had to pay an annual subscription, Md Nurul Huque did not get selected by the Labour party, they were very strict about it, but that did not stop the community from fielding the Bangladeshi candidate.

Incidently, the community's champions were not from Sylhet, but rather from Dhaka and Chittagong. They were very bright, educated, disciplined, married with noble standing in the community in East London, and also in Bangladesh, in their respective area.

Purbo & Poshchim Alee

I will just touch the surface here. In a conversation with an ex-councillor and elder of mine, he re-told me the matters of the past, how the Bangladeshi community in Tower Hamlets was set up, the divided community.

East & West. Pubalees = Eastenders and pochimalees = Westenders, east being pubalee which consists of the Cannon St. Rd area and west being pochimalee and this consisted of Brick Lane and surrounding area.

So the pubalees, were people from the Sylhet regions of Biswanath, Jagannath puri and pochimalees, were people from the other parts of Sylhet regions such as Balagoinj, Moulovibazar where the tribal dynamics of the time were and this is how the community moved with political issues.

This would have had a bearing on the results of 1982 as well as the dynamics of the groups, the region groups would have stuck together and as such there would have been a tsunami of trepedations within the groups that would have determined who got how many votes. Those that were there who wanted to pursue their political aspiration, as independent councillors, they either did not agree and support the community elder's decisions, and broke rank, or those who simply thought they'll take their chances. This illustrates the disunity and also harmony in the community, an oxymoronic time.

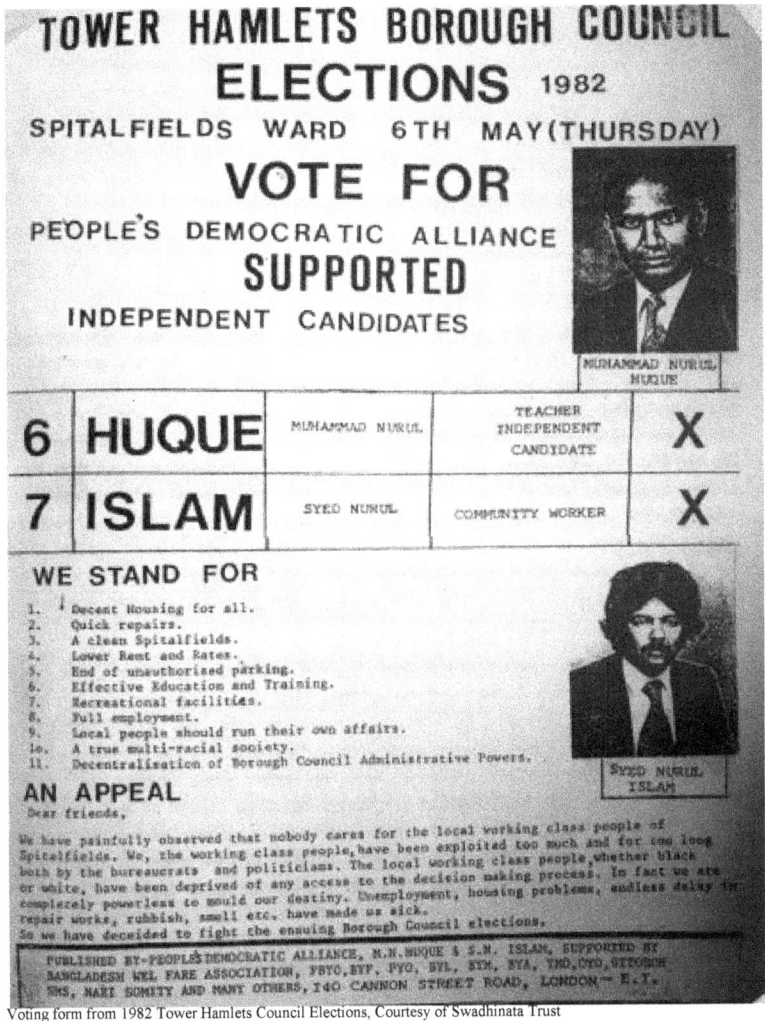

Voting form from 1982 Tower Hamlets Council Elections, Courtesy of Swadhinata Trust

These are the two candidates chosen by the People's Democratic Alliance (PDA)

Earliest Political Pioneers

These are the first results of the Bangladeshi candidates who contested seats for the first time in Tower Hamlets.

The Bangladesh Welfare Association (BWA) and other voluntary organisations were mobilised to get the candidates prepared and ready to enter into the mainstream Politics. They took the steps to be heard and seen and counted. The move from voluntary organisation to a government body, to be part of the policy making, shaping and enforcing.

Majority of the community vanguards had already experienced and been on the receiving end of tokenism, hollow words and promises; and been let down too many times. The community was being used and after the death of Altab Ali in 1978, enough was enough, Bangladeshis were capable of taking their place in the driving seat.

Result from 1982-1986 Pathfinders

Ward	Year	Name	Party	Votes
St Katharine's	1982	Md. A Ali	Lab	1123
		Shahab Uddin Ahmed	Ind	185
		Md. A. Hague	Ind	65
St Mary's	1982	Rofique Ullah	SDP	205
Spitalfields	1982	Md Nurul Huque	Ind	638
		Syed Nurul Islam	Ind	530
		Md. Gulam. Mustafa	SDP	407
		Abdul Gofur	Ind	173
		Sirajul Hoque	Ind	157
Weavers	1982	Md. A. Hussain	Ind	246

The above table indicates the year and ward of the first Bangladeshi contestants standing for councillorship.

The Break through

The councillors of 1982 Md Nurul Huque and Md Ashik Ali were the breakthrough that the community pinned their hopes on. They were to help and relieve the plight of the community. These two set the cogs in motion in the council chambers.

1982 - 1986

	Md Nurul Huque		
Spitalfields		Ind	638

Muhammad Nurul Huque was the community's "Golden Boy," he was chosen to champion the community, a community that invested all its energy, resources and manpower to challenge the then Labour party. His win sent a shockwave to the Labour party, the moment had "bulldozed", the party's stance on the Bangladeshis of Spitalfields and greater Tower Hamlets.

	M Ashik Ali		
St Katharine's		Lab	1123

Changing the status of squatters and also changing the perception of the community. The perception then was that the Bangladeshi community were free loaders and will not pay their way.

The councillors had to get the council to give the squatters,"tenant status with rent books and re-housing those that live in inhabitable housing."

This was still a slow process and took many years under the then Lib Dem council's leadership.

1982's

1982 was the year of the Bangladeshi community that launched its political campaign to integrate within the wider community on the power sharing platform. The community mobilised itself and put forward a selection of candidates.

1. Md Nurul Huque1982 - Independent
2. Late Md Ashik Ali 1982 Labour
3. Late Shahab Uddin Ahmed (Belal) 1982 - Independent
4. Shirazul Hoque 1982- Labour
5. Helal Uddin Abbas -1985- Labour
6. Late Jahangir (Jan) Alam1986- Labour
7. Late Md Sadique Ahmed 1986- Labour
8. Shunwar Ali 1986- Labour
9. Akikur Rahman 1986 - SDP
10. Salim Ullah 1986 - Labour
11. Ghulam Mortuza 1986 – Labour

The above named persons were the contenders of the 80s who became a councillor or went on to become one later. The 80s was a furtile time for the Bangladeshi community to "root" in the borough as the seeds were sawn in the 1970s.

We had Bangladeshi contestants but strikingly noticeable is one Labour, two SDP and no Conservatives. It was clear from these facts that the 'working class socialist' Labour party wasn't for the Bangladeshi community at that time.

The number of independent contestants indicates the political discourse that the Bangladeshi community had with the parties. They were clearly not meeting nor addressing the Bangladeshi community's needs. No party was representing the Bangladeshi community or was investing in the people. From the squallors of the 70's to the overcrowdings of the 80's. The Bangladeshi community endured hardships and inequalities under British citizenship without a voice.

The Spitalfields ward election 1982

Spitalfield		
Year	Electorate	Turnout (%)
1982	4,873	35.8
Name	Party	Votes
Mohammed Nurul Huque	Ind	638

Mrs A Elboz	Lab	560
Ms S.M. Carlyle	Lab	556
Syed Nurul Islam	CW	530
S. Corbishley	Lab	496
W. Kelly	SDP	417
Muhammed Gulam Mustafa	SDP	407
G.G.N. White	SDP	401
Abdul Gofur	Ind	173
Sherajul. Hoque	Ind	157

So on the day about 1750 people came out to vote and the votes were split fourways, The top firsts of each group, Nurul Hoque Ind. (638), Elboz Labour (560), Kelly SDP (417), and another independent, (135 or so).

If the other three independent candidates did not contest then the community elders backed candidate would have won by a big majority, he would have got additional 860 votes, making his grand total votes of 1,498.

This [would have] made a seismic tectonic shift in the politics of Tower Hamlets as the wining result would have resonated into a water tight community, the Labour party and the Sylheti community but the nature of the Sylheti community as it was, inherently acted against the patriachy that lead us to have more than three divides.

Another point to highlight here, this is one of the times that the patriarchy was challenged, disobeyed and undermind. This was a radical act from the young men who stood in the election. Standing in the election would have been a direct front to the patriachy. This would also signify that the elders were losing "absolute control" grip of the integrated young men who were being groomed by key vanguards local agencies.

It is clear to see that Syed Nurul Islam received decent votes and if the community elders backed him, he could have won, this was the year for the Bangladeshis in local politics. Here we have couple of elements at play, one being that the sizeable votes he got, he had 530 votes, he was 500 strong so he would have entered the race on the knowledge of that; he will have been supported and fronted by the "Pubalee & Poshimalee" at play. This also highlights that there were more than one patriarchy at play.

From the research information gathered from interviews, it appears that Syed Nurul Islam did not make the first choice, it was because of an array of reasons and some were radical; he was young and he was assimilated into the indegenious community. His attitude and practises were not supported by the elders as they were seen as radical, he wasn't someone they could endorse as he wasn't in-tune with the status quo of the elders, he was known to socialise and was active in the new growing sub-cultures that were unfolding within the youth of the Bangladeshi community; and on those basis as well as other "Deshi" derogotary reasons too, discrimination by the community's elites, will have focused on their backgrounds and class were factors taken into account in the selection process by the elders.

Mohammed Gulam Mustafa with the Social Democratic Party (SDP) also got sizeable vote. This would have given confidence to the people of the wards and community, the rejoicing of the fact that they tasted their first opportunity, the chance to choose an individual from amongst themselves – representation of the people by the people, after decades of being choiceless of their kind. We can clearly see the release because of the number of people who put themselves forward as candidates and then winning.

On another front there were developments taking place in the local Labour Political party. There were people from all over the country were verging into Tower Hamlets. This was changing the minds in the local Labour party – from a racist one to more open to the plight of the Bangladeshi community.

Jill Cove and her partner George encountered similar problems entering into the Labour party, who then championed the cause and perserviered till a point when it presented itself when there were three Labour members were there in the meeting, giving them [Jill] a quorum. Jill and the other members took the decision to open the membership up. According to the notes in Sarah Glynns book, soon after Helal Abbas and others, Ala Uddin I believe became paid up members.

Phil Maxwell

In 1982 Phil Maxwell entered into Tower Hamlets politics from Liverpool. He was a Labour left member in the Spitalfields ward.

He recollects the political environment of the time, while Spitalfields has the highest concentration of Bangladeshis; there were not many members and no representatives on the council.

> *"Bethnal green constituency Labour Party - which I was a delegate to -they use to meet at the Bethnal green town hall.*
> *The first meeting I went to of the Labour party was the Spitalfields ward LP meeting – there were hardly any*

Bangladeshi members – it was obvious to me and others – that there was some kind of instutionalised rascism going on – and there were, it was predominantly white, and when you think about it – the Bangladeshi community at that time –really concentrated in Spitalfields around there and the reason for that was that – because it was considered fairly safe place away from chances of experiencing racial abuse or actual racist attack."

There was an attitude I remember that some people thought that
Well, their English isn't very good, so how can they possible be suitable as council candidate

But they didn't look at in a different way which they should have
well, they're bilingual they at least speak two languages. And obviously lot of the Bangladeshi had come over only for few years they will be improving with their English.

I don't agree with this idea and it was prevalent at the time 'That they can't speak English very well so they can't be councillors.'

What you got to remember is the Bangladeshi community was hugely underrepresented by Bangladeshi members. It was important and there was a lot of people that time.

The situation obviously changed now so you needed to have political representative, of course you do of the Bangladeshi community.

So the arguments that we used to prevent, Bangladeshi becoming councillors were "specious," what we will call it institutionalised racisms today. There was a lot of that."

The Third Pathfinder

Three years later our 3rd joined pathfinders, Mr Helal Uddin Abbas.
1985 -1986

Spitalfields	Helal Uddin Abbas	Lab	638

Three years on in 1985 the third person was elected in a local byelection, Helal Uddin Abbas in Spitalfields.

Helal Uddin Abbas was a paid up member of the Labour party and the party would have taken a swift decision to front him and give him the full support.

"His long experience of the 'problems faced by the local people' in the ward enabled him to 'represent the interests of all members of the community on the council' – particular stuggles involving homeless families."

The winning of the 1982 election in Spitalfields was a clear statement by the community to the wider one and alarm bells to the political parties. This also showed how the community got behind the elections and voted. The tactics and strategies that were used to insure a Bangladeshi win. The community were getting knowledgeable and wiser and this facilitated growth.

"Political participation is inherent within the Bangladeshi community; even a child at primary school level is politically aware and active in Bangladesh."

This would have been seen as another breakthrough for the community on many levels:
- that the Labour party succumbed
- the realisation of power
- experience of power
- that the elders with the community effected change,
- benefit of unity within the local election setting
- that a Sylheti "true" representation
- A son of Sylhet got elected

So the new locally educated young men who were mentored by Shaha Lutfur Rahman and Abdul Aziz and others, weere these individuals who got themselves in position, which, itself was a front to the patriachy. So as we transitioned to 1986 general election, the membership of Helal Uddin Abbas and his win in 1985 will have opened the doors to the local Labour party membership.

To have this position will have given the individuals power and authority over the patriarchy when it comes the local Labour party politics. This will have created new dynamics. The elders will have to concede some of the patriachy leverage and accept the new found position and recognise the individual for the sake of the community's progress. This will have created an even playing field for the one who wears the "local Labour elected hat" who is the "gateway," to what the community has been seeking.

The yielding of absolute power 1982 by the elders was short lived, practically for three years, because from 1985, Labour were processing the people and putting them forward for candidacy.

> "The selection of Abbas Uddin, a radical young Bangladeshi community worker, was seen by Labour Party activists as a public declaration of their anti-racist credential."

So the elders were not selecting the party candidates; that, took away their power to influence at the local party level; the political party and their members were selecting and choosing the candidates. This gave the Bengali councillors a bubble of protection, in particular the accessibility and connection to the Labour party facility; there is also another bubble that comes at the council is the service and facility that othered, such as resources, facility and personal development.

These wins will have had chain reactions and the ramifications far, wide and deep. The community will have worked like ants, so many lines and layers will have been at work on so many levels, strategising and building the community.

I came across this a section in Pnina & Muhammad's book, making references to the impact it had on the elders after the 1985 by-election in Spitalfields and boroughwide.

> "Between 1982-1986 vigourous rivalry among prominent figures within Bangladeshi pressure groups influenced certain struggles in the political arena. Older businessmen,

> *predominantly from Sylhet, who held posts in the largest and oldest community group, the Bangladesh Welfare Association (BWA), encountered stiff opossitionfrom the Sylheti second generation activists who were mostly linked to the various youth recreational groups. These younger leaders have established a national platform through Federation of Bangladeshi Youth organisation (FBYO)".*

The trio would have sent a clear message to the core community activists that the Bangladeshi community was in and the know-how was there to enable many others to follow. These affects of the experiences and knowledge can be seen and analysed in the progression of the community in the boroughs politics.

The trio will have made in-roads in the council chamber, the plight of the community will have been presented formally in the council meetings where they will have been documented, thus giving the community a "voice," and where the voice of the community had to be heard, the act itself of councillors representation and presentations the community and its plight in the council chambers, the council bound by it's policies to afford the community legitimacy that it denied and from that point on give it credibility.

Since then we can see the positives as well as the negatives; the positives being that the Bangladeshi community was alive and kicking and taking their seat in the decision making arena. The negative is that a particular group became exclusive which affected everyone the opportunity to pursue their political career; divide and rule, personal career goals and some power tripping.

The next two decades 1982-1998, four election terms; 20 years, the community saw the councillorship grow and grow. We did well to secure two councillors in 1982 and then to go on and to become dominant force but the community still wasn't ready for the transition to the MP-ship, as it is still in its local government political infancy. Greater planning and education was needed to prepare the community to present, represent and vote for the results to get to the House of Parliament.

The two decades were significantly and inherently different and can be split into two, the 80s & 90s. The 80s was the foundation setting during what seemed ancient and alien times where the pathfinder lead the way, and the 2nd terms they became the pioneers and paved the way for the 90s instalments.

They bore so much, the gravity, the weight, the emergency, the urgency that the community invested in the councillors. Yet, it is not clear as to what hostility and stonewalling they received as a minority in the council chambers and the prejudices of their oppositions.

There is a lot that can be gauged from the services that was made available by the party in power, it wasn't good, and prejudices prevailed in services on the grass root level. And from this we can take it that the three Bangladeshi councillors were against the tide, yet they insured that they got involved in the committees, where policies were discussed, reviewed, changed and made.

This is the first of council documents that hold the Bangladeshi councillor's names, though the first two were elected in 1982, this document was compiled according to the date in 1985. However, councillor Helal Uddin Abbas was elected in 1985 in a byelection in Spitalfields. His name was added afterwards by hand.

Official Document: List of elected members

LIST OF MEMBERS 1985/86

ABEL, Donald Joseph	William Guy Gardens, Talwin Street, E3
ALI, Mian Mohammed Asheek	Kindersley House, Pinchin Street, E1 1RR (Phone: 481-2968 (P))
ALLEN, Graham	8, Cressy House, Hannibal Road, E1 3JT (Phone: 790-0566 (P))
APPIAN, Kofi Bakor	Chambord Street, E2 7NJ (Phone: 729-4803 (P))
ARNOTT, (Mrs) Eva	Sheridan House, Tarling Street, E1 2PB (Phone: 790-7618 (P))
ARNWHISTLE, Robert William	Woollon House, Clark Street, E1 3XZ (Phone: 790-2542 (P))
AYLMER, Peter Donald	Anson House, Duckett Street, E1 4BB (Phone: 791-0622 (P); 555-3331 (B) and 633-6960 (Messages))
BEASLEY, Paul	Whitethorn Street, E3 4DA (Phone: 987-5537 (P))
BEER, Reginald	Garford Street, E14 8JC (Phone: 515-9190 (P); 987-1883 (B))
FLOUNDERS, Eric	Tredegar Square, E3 5AN (Phone: 981-3156 (P); 930-4321 x 264 (B))
GOODCHILD, Andrew Robert	(A) Damien Court, Damien Street, E1 2EL
GUY, William Thomas George	Priory Street, E3 3BU (Phone: 980-6416 (P))
HEARN, Jennifer Anne	Mile End Road, E1 (Phone: 790-3383 (P); 377-2521 (B))
HEWISON, (Miss) Elizabeth (M.B.E.)	Westbrook House, Victoria Park Square, E2 (Phone: 980-5581 (P))
HOLMES, Benjamin	Union Drive, Canal Close, Solebay Street, E1 (Phone: 790-5885 (P))
HUGHES, Peter James	Mackworth Point, Rainhill Way, E3
HUQUE, Muhammad Nurul	Buxton Street, E1
KELLY, Daniel	Elderfield House, West India Dock Road, E14 (Phone: 987-5924 (P); 985-3388 (B))
KILGOUR, William Charles Mackie	Alastor House, Strattondale Street, E14 9UF (Phone: 987-5802 (P))
SMALLWOOD, (Mrs) Jeanette Patricia	Alderney Road, E1 4EG
STREETER, Patrick Thomas	Cressy House, Hannibal Road, E1 3JT (Phone: 790-5965 (P); 0279-721308 (B))
UDDIN, Abbas	Creulock Rise Crealock Street
THOMPSON, (Mrs) Patricia Mary	Brownfield Street, E14 6ND (Phone: 987-7542 (P))
TWOMEY, Dennis	Brokesley Street, E3 4QL (Phone: 980-6468 (P))
WILLIAMS, Brian	Tredegar Square, E3 5AE (Phone: 981-3156 (P))

Courtesy of the Tower Hamlets Archive Library

Following documents shows the roles the first two Bangladeshi councillors took/given.

STANDING COMMITTEES OF THE COUNCIL 1985/86

1. **ADMINISTRATION COMMITTEE**
   Councillors Abel, Ashkettle, Catchpole(Mrs), Day (Mrs), Durell, Flounders, Mudd, O'Neill, Saunders and Streeter.

2. **AMENITIES COMMITTEE**
   Councillors Armsby (Mrs), Aylmer, Curran (Mrs), Desmond, Kilgour, Ludlow, Ramanoop, Smallwood (Mrs), Streeter and Thompson (Mrs).

3. **DEVELOPMENT COMMITTEE**
   Councillors Abel, Beer, Chaney, Cowley, Durell, Huque, Ludlow, Ramanoop, Saunders and Shaw.

4. **FINANCE COMMITTEE**
   Councillors Armsby (Mrs), Ashkettle, Beer, Duffey, Guy, Hewison (Miss), Price, Saunders, Shanahan and Streeter. (One vacancy)

5. **HEALTH AND CONSUMER SERVICES COMMITTEE**
   Councillors Appiah, Aylmer, Catchpole (Mrs), Durell, Huque, Kilgour, O'Neill, Ramanoop, Smallwood (Mrs) and Thompson (Mrs).

6. **POLICY COMMITTEE**
   Councillors Ashkettle, Chaney, Desmond, Downes, Flounders, Guy, Holmes, Mudd, O'Neill, Penner, and Twomey.

In the portion we can see Mr Huque was in the 3. Development Committee & 5. Health and Consumer Services Committee.

7. **SOCIAL SERVICES COMMITTEE**
   Councillors Abel, Armsby, Carlyle, Hearn, Hewison (Miss), Holmes, Kilgour, Lebar, Shaw and Thompson (Mrs).

8. **HOUSING MANAGEMENT COMMITTEE**
   Councillors Abel, Ali, Beer, Carlyle, Day (Mrs), Goodchild, Hughes, Rackley, Shanahan and Thompson (Mrs).

In this portion we can see Mr Ali was on the - 8. Housing management Committee.

9. **ETHNIC MINORITIES COMMITTEE**
   Councillors Ali, Cowley, Curran (Mrs), Downes, Huque, Penner, Price, Rackley and Shanahan. (One vacancy)

10. **WORKS COMMITTEE**
    Councillors Aylmer, Beer, Cowley, Duffey, Flounders, Kilgour, Lilley and Williams (One vacancy)

11. **POLICE COMMITTEE**
    Councillors Hearn, Hughes, Huque, Price and Twomey. (Five vacancies)

12. **SPECIAL TRANSFER COMMITTEE**
    Councillors Appiah, Ashkettle, Carlyle, Chaney, Goodchild, Guy, Kelly, Lilley, Mudd, Penner, Riley and Streeter.

13. **SPECIAL (ORGANISATION AND STRUCTURES) COMMITTEE**
    Chairman and Vice-Chairman of Administration Committee.
    Chairman of Finance Committee.
    Leader of the Council (or his nominee).
    Chairman of Council & Staff (Officers) Joint Sub-Committee (Employers Side).

In this portion we see Mr Ali and Mr Hoque also on 9. Ethnic Minority Committee as well as on 11. Police Committee.

According to this list Mr Hoque had committed himself to his role as a councillor; he has put himself in all the places where the community needed urgent attention.

The integral roles that were taken by Mr Ali and Mr Hoque proved to be where the cogs of change for the community on a formal level begun. They both bore the burden of the community and knew the weight it carried, its expectations, especially of Mr Hoque, the people's choice in Spitalfields.

Both of them knew the weight that burdened on their shoulders, minds and hearts; they were the "Community Champions," sent forth; the pressure must have been immense for both; yet without a doubt Nurul Haque would have had a daunting and far challenging time as he did not have backing from a political party as Ashik Ali did.

1985

After Mrs A Elboz, Labour councillor in Spitalfields died, a byelection took place where Labour put Helal Uddin Abbas.

This was the local political game changer for the party as well as the local people. Double edged – while the community was getting what it always dreamed of – inclusion into the party and on the other hand the silencing of the the elders achievement of challenging the parties with their know-how of getting Independent candidates elected.

As a paid up member Helal Abbas was Labour party recognising the error they made and how the party to capitalise and re-address on what had unfolded in 1982. It was a tsunami that came over Tower Hamlets; even though Liberals capitalised for the next four years.

So, Helal Abbas being selected as the Labour candidate in Spitalfields, this took out the power of the sting from the community elders, those who exercised their power in selecting the local candidates in 1982. It meant that the elders were relegated but that would be counter productive to the party and Helal Abbas.

We can see from the following general election results that there were no independent councillors elected. Md Nurul Huque did stand again as an Independent but did not get elected like he was supported in 1982; he came 4th

out of 11 contesting in 1986. It was so bad that he had to join the Liberals Democrats in 1994 to have a standing in the local political arena, again he came 4th out of 7 contesting the Spitalfields ward.

We see here what has happened for Md Nurul Huque, the people's champion of 1982. The Labour party did not have him as a member so he could not become a Labour Councillor. The local party dynamics were at work; so what happened to the Bangladeshi community before they were allowed to become members.

While Md Nurul Huque was supported by the core elders in 1982 but by 1986 there was a new champion in town, as many people will have naturally gravitated to the Labour candidates, it was a matter of prestige and credibility for the community groups. Labour party endorsement was the prize that was alway on their sight. Helal Uddin Abbas became the second Labour councillor and the first Sylheti one.

It is the case that the elder worked closely with Peter Shore MP at the time and they were vying to get a footing in the local Labour party membership. However, we can see that there was no political development there. Under Peter Shore MP-ship, inclusion in the the local Labour camp did not come quick or easy.

So, the people's champion Nurul Huque did serve a purpose but after that he never won, to continue to champion the community that title swiftly shifted to Helal Uddin Abbas. Mr Nurul Huques political career in Spitalfields was sealed in 1985 when Helal Abbas won.

> *"Somewhat peversley, the PDA could not resist putting up their own candidate, who squeezed the Labour majority down to just nine votes."*
>
> Page 150 of Sarah Glynn's book

> *"When Abbas Uddin was selected by the ward Labour Party to fight the 1985 by-election, Nurul Huque assisted the campaign of Abbas Uddin's most dangerous rival, Abdul Hannan, who stood as an independent having left the ward Labour Party after a power struggle with its white left-wing and Bangladeshi leaders."*
>
> Page 63 of Pnina Werbner & Muhammad Anwar's book

It is clear from the previous paragraph that the elders through the PDA had the power and was going to weild their power again. They also knew the strategy, in order to build on their achievement; they need to get another independent councillor to help Cllr Md Nurul Hoque. This is seen in the energy and the effort spent to promote their candidate of 1985, Abdul Hannan. The loss was a bitter blow for Md Nurul Huque as this would have alienated him with the prevailing young second generation leaders along with the elders defeat.

However, it did not stop Nurul Huque as he continued to champion the cause for the community; he gave his personal life for the Bangladeshi East End and also in Bangladesh; in his home town where he financed a school. He still remains in the community, living in Tower Hamlets but in poor health, he is surviving cancer. While he knows that he was discriminated by certain individuals in the borough and by his own community during his active life, now many people as well wannabe councillors go to him as a respected elder and to still consult with him.

Following table compares the results between 1982 & 1986

Year	Electo rates	Turnout %	Candi dates	Bengali contender	Nurul Huque [won]	Nurul Islam	Gulam Mostafa
1982	4873	35.8 [3128]	10	5	638	530	407

Year	Electo rates	Turnout %	Candi dates	Bengali contender	Helal U Abbas	Gulam Mortuza	Nurul Huque [4th]
1986	5648	45.2 [3096]	11	6	1246	1019	837

In 1986 we can see from the figures the shape of the result. Even though Nurul Huque mirrors hit vote figure from 638 to 837, getting more votes then 1982 porportionate to the electorate and the turn out. Helal Abbas was 227 vote clearly in lead from Gulam Mortuza and 409 votes from Nurul Huque; and 258 votes ahead of Phil Maxwell who came third with 988 votes.

1986 - 1990

Ward	Name	Party	Votes
St Dunstan's	Jahangir Alam	Lab	1142
St Katharine's	Md Ashik Ali	Lab	1562
St Katharine's	Md Sadique Ahmed	Lab	1513
Spitalfields	Helal Uddin Abbas	Lab	1246
Spitalfields	Md Gulam Mortuza	Lab	1019

The 80s were formidable years for the Bangladeshi community living in Tower Hamlets under the Liberal majority council. These five councillors and the three senior councillors had so much to do. The weight of the whole community rested on their shoulders.

The growth of Bangladeshi Councillors bar chart

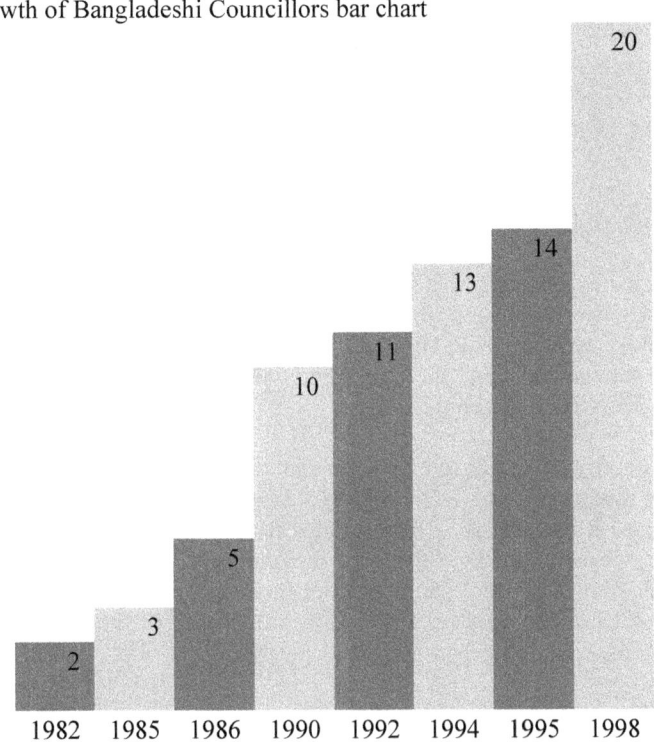

The three new councillors, well versed community champions that had no time to lose as they had so much to do, so much to change and so many lives to empower. Where do you start, it doesn't matter which direction you look at in terms of the service, conditions of living and quality of life, everything needed to be reviewed, assessed and adopted to meet the needs of the community. The new found opportunity and power to change the Bangladeshi peoples' lives and from within, changed the local authority's attitude and prejudices in servicing us and fulfilling the community's needs. After the Liberals came into power in Tower Hamlets, they de-centralised the services and introduced 'one-stop shops' in every ward, and this was the first time I became aware of accessing council services.

While it was great having these one stop shops in your locality, the service and experiences were very bad to disgraceful, my personal account of being left to wait for a long time before being seen only to be talked down to. The quality of care and respect wasn't there, especially for the elderly who could not speak English well, the children had to translate best as possible and also were in the front line for receiving the poor to apathetical attitudes from the estate officers and receptionist and other frontline workers.

Latter part of the 80s, midway into the 1986 election there were visible changes being witnessed at these one stop shops. The council started recruiting Bangladeshi workers and interpreters were being employed and made available to help the elders and non English speaking residents.

The community slowly got their voice through the councillors, the people were now channelling their grievance through the representatives and the officers were being made to be accountable. So many other policy changes had been implemented and the community was being nourished and signs of the positive outcomes could be seen.

The community no longer felt invisible and ignored, they now had a voice and a process they could go through. They were no longer isolated, they were being recognised and afforded the services that they are entitled to. This was the early days of the cogs moving and chain reaction taking effect, but, still there were many miles to go before any signs of equality, fairness and justice could be seen in the distribution of the services and resources that were in the borough for its people.

1990

St Dunstan's	Shahab Uddin. Ahmed (Belal)	Lab	1628
St Katharine's	Abdul Asad	Lab	2028
St Katharine's	Rajan Uddin Jalal	Lab	1951
St Katharine's	Shirazul Haque	Lab	1931
St Peter's	Abdul Rohim	Lib	1981
Shadwell	Mrs Pola Manzila. Uddin	Lab	1447
Spitalfields	Gulam Mortuza	Lab	1482
Spitalfields	Helal Uddin Abbas	Lab	1451
Weavers	Sajjad Miah	Lib	2335
Holy Trinity	Akikur Rahman	Lib	1688

1992 By-Elections

| Spitalfields | Syed A Mizan | Lab | 1098 |

1994

Holy Trinity	Nuruddin Ahmed	Lab	1407
Limehouse	Soyful Alom	Lab	1559
St Dunstan's	Md Shahab Uddin	Lab	1965

St Katharine's	Abdul Asad	Lab	2131
St Katharine's	Rajan Uddin Jalal	Lab	2020
St Mary's	Bodrul M Alom	Lab	1560
St Peter's	Ala Uddin	Lab	2010
Shadwell	Mrs Pola M. Uddin	Lab	1652
Shadwell	Abdus Shukur	Lab	1635
Spitalfields	Syed A Mizan	Lab	1937
Spitalfields	Gulam Mortuza	Lab	1864
Spitalfields	Ataur Rahman	Lab	1740
Weavers	Sunawar Ali	Lab	1518

1995 By-Elections

Weavers	Mohammed Ali	Lab	1388

1998

Blackwall	Kumar Murshid	Lab	691
Bromley	Abdul Aziz Sardar	Lab	1504
East India	Rajib Ahmed	Lab	790
Holy Trinity	Salim Ullah	Lab	1314
Limehouse	Helal Uddin Abbas	Lab	928
Limehouse	Soyful Alom	Lab	771
Redcoat	Ataur Rahman	Lab	992
St Dunstan's	Shahab Uddin Ahmed	Lab	1231
St Dunstan's	Mohammed Shahab Uddin	Lab	1220
St Katharine's	Abdul Asad	Lab	1496
St Katharine's	Anamul Haque	Lab	1333
St Mary's	Motin Uz-Zaman	Lab	826
St Peter's	Jusna Begum	Lab	1405
St Peter's	Raja Miah	Lab	1223
Shadwell	Bodrul M Alom	Lab	1229
Shadwell	Abdus Shukur	Lab	1112
Spitalfields	Syed A Mizan	Lab	1454
Spitalfields	Gulam Mortuza	Lab	1435
Spitalfields	Ala Uddin	Lab	1316
Weavers	Mohammed Ali	Lab	1229

Uncontested Areas

Bow			
Lansbury			
Millwall			
Park			

Above areas were not contested until 1998.

This shows that we had low numbers of Bangladeshi residents living in the area or white dominated area where Bangladeshi contestants would not get a vote from the residents.

This is very clear from the 1982 candidates where the community had to put up independent councillors and only one candidate was from Labour and one from Social Democratic Party. There were no Liberal Bangladeshi candidates or Conservatives at the time.

As we follow the information tabled for each election term we can see the shifts and changes, how the political environment was getting shaped. Two elections later even the liberals had to recruit Bangladeshi candidates.

The Bangladeshi community entered into the political arena without the Parties. The community succeeded in securing an independent councillor and the people meant business, the future was only going to get better.

The community learnt that the local political parties were managed by local people and they determined who got selected. The community decided to do something about this; they started getting actively involved in the parties and started networking with the community and recruiting members.

The community needed a voice in the local party offices where candidate selection process takes place; however our Bengali community didn't get selected until 1982, remedying this was a long term plan but the short term actions needed to be taken. I recollect becoming a member as soon as I turned 18 and became part of the bolstering of the Bangladeshi membership.

This drive also changed the internal workings of the local parties, and in turn, many local party personnel's became supportive of developing the community's political aspirations.

We know from the data that in 1986 we had a massive increase in the elected councillors and the increase in Labour contestants. The community was full of resilient activists, aspiring politicians and leaders who were striving and hungry to thrust the community's needs forward and inherently theirs. Amongst them there were many aspiring young men. However, only few were educated and had professional background; many were from various backgrounds and many of them educated themselves by taking up English for Speakers of Other Languages (ESOL) classes in the evenings set up by key vanguards through local organisations, such as Avenues Unlimited, Toc H and St Mary's centre.

St Katharine's Ward

St Katharine's ward was one of the first wards to have a Bangladeshi councillor, a ward where, the Labour party put their first Bangladeshi candidate. This was a historic moment for the community from the Labour party perspective and the other is the fact that the community took on the political parties on.

So putting Barister Ashik Ali was a strategic move by the local Labour party; for them to capitalise on the sentiments and the rawness of the death of a resident of Wapping, tenant of Reardon House, Altab Ali. Labour accepted, supported and put forward Barrister Md Ashik Ali, a resident of Wapping.

The Labour party would have had four years in the making of the Bangladeshi members into a candidate, with full knowledge of the issues, tensions and expectations of the Bangladeshi community. It is also the case that the word on the street would have been that the community was mobilising itself, and it would have been a bad move for the Labour party not to put forward a Bangladeshi candidate.

If the Labour party knowing this did not respond, to not put a Bangladeshi candidate forward and the community went with an independent candidate, the independent candidate would have won, just like Mohammed Nurul Hoque did in Spitalfields ward. It is clear that St Katharine's & Spitalfields wards were highly populated with politically active voters from the Bangladeshi community.

This stronghold over St Katharine's ward was kept for many terms until the boundary changes began, and the number of seats reduced. This changed the election dynamics and the stronghold was lost in 2014 when the Labour party did not put a Bangladeshi candidate, Labour came second with one seat.

So between 1982-2014 St Katharine's ward was a safe haven for Bangladeshi councillors. The ward had seen many Bangladeshi councillors and many of whom won repeatedly, and amongst them was Councillor Abdul Asad.

The community has come a long way and the political journey has transformed the community and its political aspiration. It is clear after a decade of politics the community had learnt so much that it ventured out to form independent groups such as the Respect party, Tower Hamlets First (THT) and recently the People's Alliance Tower Hamlets (PATH).

These groups were better suited to the issues of the community that had transitioned and had an impact on the main parties. Many traditional Labour party members changed to become one of the latter. It's the original game changer party, George Galloway's Respect Party which ousted Oona King in the 2008 election during the Middle East war which further fuelled the popularity decline of the party.

So the relationship of the Labour stronghold ward has seen demise in the Bangladeshi councillorship. There clearly is a rift in the party members of the ward who don't value the party line. Especially for Abdul Asad who was Labour councillor in St Katharine's ward had changed allegence to another party. So in the 2014 local elections after 32 years there were no Bangladeshi Labour candidates or from any of the other main parties, only one from Tower Hamlets First who came fifth. The Conservatives won two seats and Denise Jones too for the Labour party who like Abdul Asad "**was**" St Katharine's ward.

It will be interesting to see why there is such a dramatic change; a strong Labour stronghold had now fallen to the Conservatives. Is it because of issues with the party, issues with the party councillors on a local level, or is it that there has been a gentrification process taking place and the demographics have changed? It could also be the case that the infighting amongst the community's political giants has a ramification on the results.

Following table consists of the election results of St Katharine's ward from 1982 – 2014, so that we have an overview at a glance.

St Katherine's		
Year	**Electorate**	**Turnout (%)**
1982	7,235	35.3
Name	**Party**	**Votes**
Md. Asik. Ali	Lab	1123
G.W. Allen	Lab	1096
J.R Ramanoop	Lab	946

St Katherine's		
Year	**Electorate**	**Turnout (%)**
1986	8,668	34.9
Name	**Party**	**Votes**
J.M. Rowe	Lab	1651
Md. Asik. Ali	Lab	1562
Md.Sadik. Ahmed	Lab	1513

St Katherine's

Year	Electorate	Turnout (%)
1990	8,987	41.4
Name	**Party**	**Votes**
Abdul Asad	Lab	2028
Rajan Uddin Jalal	Lab	1951
Shirazul Islam	Lab	1931

St Katherine's

Year	Electorate	Turnout (%)
1994	9,182	47.6
Name	**Party**	**Votes**
Abdul Asad	Lab	2131
Mrs Denise Jones	Lab	2116
Rajon Uddin Jalal	Lab	2020

St Katherine's

Year	Electorate	Turnout (%)
1998	10689	32.1
Name	**Party**	**Votes**
Mrs Denise Jones	Lab	1582
Abdul Asad	Lab	1496
Anamul Hoque	Lab	1333

St Katherine's & Wapping

Date	Electorate	Turnout (%)
2.5.2002	8508	29.76
Name	**Party**	**Votes**
Mrs Denise Jones	Lab	1082
Shafiqul Haque	Lab	1049
Richard David Brooks	Lab	1034

St Katherine's & Wapping

Date	Electorate	Turnout (%)
4.5.2006	9222	35.46
Name	**Party**	**Votes**
Dr Emma Jones	C	1351
Shafiqul Haque	Lab	1321
Mrs Denise Jones	Lab	1290

St Katherine's & Wapping		
Date	**Electorate**	**Turnout (%)**
6.5.2010	9429	62.52
Name	**Party**	**Votes**
Dr Emma Jones	C	1623
Shafiqul Haque	Lab	1455
Mrs Denise Jones	Lab	1447

St Katherine's & Wapping		
Date	**Electorate**	**Turnout (%)**
22.5.2014	8116	46.28
Name	**Party**	**Votes**
Julia Luise Dockerill	C	1278
Mrs Denise Jones	Lab	1208
Neil Anthony King	C	1156

Letting go of the bull's horn.

Back in 1978 after all that endurance, all the beatings the community had taken and then the murders; and one of them being Altab Ali, peer of the youth of the time, friends and family members of the new generation of integrated Bangladeshis growing up in the ghetto. The community maneovured into position to take the bull by the horns, shape and alter the community's future. The community had 4 years to get itself together, prepare the people to take an active role in the "body" that shapes the lives of people living in the community.

The youth of the day and the senior members of the community took on the status quo, the seniors more reluctantly than the youth. There were issues on every level and reflecting on the number of candidates from the Labour party, the party did not represent the community adequately. With this knowledge in mind the community ensured that representation in the 1982 elections would be taking matters into our won hands, through independent candidates.
The community backed the Independent councillors as well as the Bangladeshi Labour councillor. The community broke through with two councillors. Md Nurul Huque (Independent) in Spitalfields ward and Md Ashik Ali (Labour) in St Katharine's ward.

The community was not finished with the bull, and then ensured that they held it even tighter and take on many more bulls by the horn. The community had nothing to lose and everything to gain, and they got educated with support of non Bangladeshi community members.

Bangladeshi Women

The community had been politically mobilised in the borough now for over a decade and had made many gains with the male councillors with regards to policies. It became the drive for the community to now have female councillors to represent it as well external expection too. It would have taken years of planning and developing a candidate for the people of the community to see in our first female councillor. So in 1990 we saw our first of many female councillors to come.

The capacity building of the Bangladeshi women to take up political membership and affiliation and become councillors flourished in all party camps but it is the Labour party members who have done well. It's the Labour party that gave the community the platform while the Liberals were the ones that kept the community at an arms length. It is clear that the Bangladeshi Liberal candidates who got elected was due to their individual circle of people and not solely based on the parties members' votes.

First Female Councillor

Manzila Pola Uddin, Baroness Uddin,
> born 17 July 1959 is a British life peer and community activist of Bangladeshi descent, being the first Muslim and second Asian woman to sit in the Parliament of the United Kingdom. In 2009 she was included on The Guardian's Muslim Women Power List for Britain.

It took just under a decade or two terms before the community got a Bangladeshi female councillor. In 1990 Mrs Pola Manzila Uddin stood in Shadwell and got elected. Mrs Manzila won by 1447 votes coming third amongst Labour candidates and third out of the overall six candidates standing for the ward.

The ward was a two party race with just Labour and Conservative; there were no Liberal or any other party standing. It was clear that Shadwell was a strong Labour ward.

Pointing out that she came third is not to discredit, for me it indicates a pattern, that one Bangladeshi candidate was placed in a 3 seat ward from the Labour party. Throughout the Bangladeshi local voting journey there have been more than one occasion when similar situations have occurred where the Bangladeshi candidates have stood out of the three, they would alway be third place, it is as though to say, balancing out the representation, it is intermittent and some lattar results have been the other way round. Paula Uddin was deputy leader 1994-95.

It would be another two terms before the community had its second elected Bangladeshi female councillor, Jusna Begum in St Peter's ward. The community would have had two female Bangladeshi councillors, but the two times elected Councillor Mrs. Manzila became a peer in the House of Lords. This was another feat of achievement for her and the community, the councillor for Shadwell who was competent to become the community's first MP was elevated to the House of Lords, this was an elevation not even conceived in the minds of the community leaders.

This elevation for the community was a surprise, a good and pleasant surprise. However, the community still did not have its first MP.

Rushanara Ali - Finally the community had an opportunity and Labour party put forward Rushanara Ali as their candidate and there were other Independent as well as conservatives, Lib Dem candidates in 2010.

When we look at her career path it becomes clear that she had the relevant experience to take on the role, capacity building. Her career path has been listed in the "Chronicle of Sylhetis of United Kingdom," Bangladeshi East End will be recording the journey of our first female MP as a future project.

Jusna Begum - Labour councillor for St Peter's ward served one term and then she moved on to her legal profession, as a solicitor. She went on to become a well respected and a successful one.

Mumtaz Samad - Labour councillor for Millwall Ward in Docklands, sadly she didn't serve a full term and resigned due to the mistreatment she received from other councillors.

She was the only Bangladeshi woman who stood during the 2002 election. To her testament, she was the only Bangladeshi candidate and she won in a very tough ward. She is duly merited being the first Bangladeshi councillor to have been elected in Millwall; list of each ward in this book which is part of the Sylheti/Bangladeshi community.

2006 was a good year for the Bangladeshi women, as four were elected.

Anwara Ali - became a Labour councillor for the Bow West ward and received 1438 votes. She then went on to stand as a Conservative candidate in the same ward, she received 1075 votes and came 5th out of 15 contesting the ward. She now represents the Conservative party. She is also a practicing GP in the borough.

Rania Khan - became a Respect councillor for the Bromley by Bow ward with 1308 votes, and went on to win her 2nd term in the same ward with 2426 as a Labour councillor.

Lutfa Begum - became a Respect councillor for the Limehouse ward with 1099 votes, she won her 2nd as a Respect councillor for the same ward with 2139 votes. She was also given the role of deputy mayor from 2009-2010.

Shiria Khatun - became a Labour councillor for the East India & Lansbury ward, with 1461 votes, and she won her 2nd term in 2010 in the same ward by 2294 votes. Shiria went on to win her 3rd term in 2014, by which time the ward boundary had changed and became the Lansbury ward, she won with 1952 votes.

Rabina Khan - entered in to Local politics in 2010, and became a Labour councillor for the Shadwell ward with 1539 votes, she went on to win her 2nd term in 2014 in the same ward with 2199 votes, but as a Tower Hamlets First (THF) councillor, independent group.

Life after their councillorship.

Mrs Pola Manzila Uddin - Labour councillor for Shadwell ward for two terms and went on to become a Peer nominated by Tony Blair Prime minister of United Kingdom 2010. Her local and personal aspiration as well as the community's to stand as an MP was taken away from her by giving her the Peerage to the House of Lords. To all our surprise, this was a better result than expected, Baroness Uddin now has much more of a significant role than of an MP who has to run for general election to keep themselves in position.

Millwall

In 2002 we had our third Bangladeshi councillor in the toughest ward in the borough for the community and that was the Millwall ward. Again the Labour party was strong that year and Mumtaz Samad won with the Labour party, although she came third amongst her Labour colleagues. Millwall was heavily contested by 11 candidates represented three of the main group plus the British National Party (BNP) and an Independent candidate.

Millwall ward contest was between Labour and the Conservatives, the Lib Dems were out of the race, however it is note worthy that BNP managed to get 204 votes to come tenth out of eleven candidates.

This was a historic win for the Bangladeshi community especially in relation to the community's endurance of years of violent racism. It was also a historic moment and a milestone for the community that a Bangladeshi female candidate got a seat. It was a proud moment for the Bangladeshi community to have Mumtaz Samad represent them in the Millwall ward and the third Bangladeshi female councillor in the council.

Mumtaz Samad's win would have a profound legacy for the community as she would have had to be a strong and a formidable person to attain the support of many residents in the ward, a ward traditionally for the Bangladeshi community was a racist one.

Mumtaz Samad in 2002, was in third position in her winning team. She was contesting two white colleagues in a white dominated area such as Millwall.
Being third in such a ward does not detract anything for the achievement but makes me wonder if she had won because of the party voter, or both, Bengali votes for Bengali councillor.

Mumtaz Samad and Md Maium Miah will be the only Bengali councillors for Millwall, as the wards name has been changed to Canary Wharf. Millwall was a notorious ward for the Bangladeshis.

Respect Party

This was a protest vote against the Labour party and their denial of allowing the Bangladeshi community getting their first MP. George Galloway contested the Bethnal Green and Bow MP seat and won. The community through Respect Party got rid of Oona King through the great Political Party plan.

Political game plan of those movers and shakers sped up the process of getting a Bangladeshi MP. The dilemma that the party brought to the table in my opinion was that the main parties had a formidable organistion to deal with and whether to deal with the 'Muslim agenda' or the original 'Bangladeshi agenda'.

It appears that the Muslim agenda has much clout and bite as there was an international and multinational backing and support available for it. Where as for the Bangladeshi one, it wasn't the same and it sat with the Labour party; which has a central control.

The Respect Party opened a chapter in the boroughs politics and the people in it. These experiences opened the door for many new groups to form and then to contest at the ballot box.

Labours Candidate from the Bangladeshi background was sought. The Labour party had to give in and put a British Bangladeshi candidate forward in the next coming general election, and no surprise we had a British Bangladeshi Member of Parliament.

We would have had our first member of parliament back in 2010 if it wasn't for Tony Blair putting forward Oona King instead of Mrs Pola Uddin. Mrs Uddin won her prior local election and the community invested eagerly and hoped for her to be the first British Bangladeshi MP.

It was the "Will of the people" in Tower Hamlets to have a Bangladeshi Member of Parliament and this was delayed and deferred by Labour Prime Minister Tony Blair; by giving the Tower Hamlets Bangladeshi community a sweetener of a gob stopper.

Tony Blair had other ideas and promoted Mrs Pola Manzila Uddin to become a "Peer" in the House of Lords. I'm sure this was looked upon by the community as a much higher status than becoming an MP, but the fact remains the spanner in works in the pursuit of the community's political aspiration were dampened.

This delayed the community by another decade or three election terms. While this was the case, it is a wonder as to what was happening behind the scene.

After Mrs Uddin was elevated to peerage, there was Rushanar Ali working in various fields and government departments. She started off with working with Oona King as her parliamentary assistant, this gave her an insight and a first hand training and experience.

Both of these respected women were bestowed with the pathfinding role from the community, they are, and will always be the beacon for the community's future generations.

I have not expanded much on the women pathfinders as they are subject of another book, so that they get an even share of recognition, presentation, scrutiny and analysis, "Blue Peter" style.

Integration Journey into the ward politics

We can see from the tables collated as follows, they demonstrate the Bangladeshi journey into the local political arena, people's maiden voyage. This is not exclusive to just Labour party, but across all main parties.

Holy Trinity		
Year	Electorate	Turnout (%)
1986	6,836	44.7
Name	Party	Votes
S.J. Charters	L	1526
Miss B.J. Knowles	L	1445
J.P. Nudds	L	1351
M.S. Chalkley	Lab	1225
G.A Cade	Lab	1167
Salim Ullah	Lab	1025
D. Ettridge	BNP	212
A.L Norton	C	138
Ms A.M. Pedlingham	C	105

St Dunstan's		
Year	Electorate	Turnout (%)
1986	6,742	40.7
Name	Party	Votes
Ms S.M Carlyle	Lab	1227
T.F Sullivan	Lab	1191
Jahangir Alam	Lab	1142
J.P Brett-Freemna	L	1058
Ms L.A. Morpurgo	L	924
P.D. Truscott	L	911
R.S. Evans	NF	256
Ms M.A Bashford	C	241
K.R Collins	C	214

Holy Trinity (3)		
Year	Electorate	Turnout (%)
1990	6,613	49.9
Name	Party	Votes
John Nudds	L Dem	1965
Jonathon Stokes	L Dem	1909
Akikur Rahman	L Dem	1688
Edward Caunter	Lab	975
Sunahwar Ali	Lab	958

Rosemary Maher	Lab	954
Stephen Smith	BNP	290
Christine Law	G	222

St Dunstan's		
Year	Electorate	Turnout (%)
1990	6,421	45.8
Name	**Party**	**Votes**
J.R Biggs	Lab	1733
D.J Gadd	Lab	1630
Shahab Uddin Ahmed	Lab	1628
T.J.B Cowley	L Dem	808
Ms C.M McNair	L Dem	751
J.S Randall	L Dem	673
D. England	GP	190
R.J Ingram	C	163
Ms S-J. Quinlan	C	138
M. Martyn	C	129

Shadwell		
Year	Electorate	Turnout (%)
1990	6,241	38.1
Name	**Party**	**Votes**
A.R. Lilley	Lab	1679
J. Riley	Lab	1575
Mrs P.M. Uddin	Lab	1447
N.D. Martin	C	574
Mrs I.J.R. Taylor	C	507
T.M. Taylor	C	507

Limehouse		
Year	Electorate	Turnout (%)
1994	5191	54.3
Name	**Party**	**Votes**
D.J. Edgar	Lab	1592
J.P. Ryan	Lab	1562
S. Alom	Lab	1559
M. Caplan	L Dem	989
Ms G. Lee	L Dem	886
S.G. Rayment	L Dem	858
P.A. Goodman	C	109
M.T Khan	Ind	98
H.C Smith	C	88
S Samih	C	71

Millwall		
Date	Electorate	Turnout (%)
2.5.2002	9302	21.98
Name	**Party**	**Votes**

Alan Thomas Amos	Lab	1089
Betheline Chattopadhyay	Lab	986
Mumtaz Samad	Lab	970
Philip William Groves	C	446
Paul William Eric Ingham	C	422
Alison Louise Newton	C	420
Malcolm James Magregor Cuthbert	L Dem	313
Jean Stokes	L Dem	245
Ian Kevin McDonald	L Dem	241
Gordon Tom Callow	BNP	204
Susan Gibson	Ind	200

Bow West		
Date	Electorate	Turnout (%)
6.5.2010	9183	65.25
Name	Party	Votes
Alan Jackson	Lab	2206
Joshua Peck	Lab	2096
Anwar Khan	Lab	2070
Sharon Bench	L Dem	1260
Anwara Ali	C	1075
Jainal Choudhury	L Dem	992
Raymond Warner	L Dem	783
Francesca Emma-louise Preece	C	723
Nicholas William Huddart	C	662
Janice Dawn Cartwright	G	576
Syed Islam	Respect	574
Aliatair James Polson	G	473
Chris Smith	G	464
Kay Ballard	Respect	356
Terry Mcgrenera	Ind	111

Millwall		
Date	Electorate	Turnout (%)
6.5.2010	DNA	DNA
Name	Party	Votes
Zara Davis	C	2959
David Snowdon	C	2693
Md Maium Miah	C	2519
John Christian Cray	Lab	2180
Doros Ullah	Lab	1943
Garry Wykes	Lab	1664
John Francis Denniston	L Dem	1362
Iain Kenedy Porter	L Dem	1177
George McFarlane	L Dem	1099
Shuily Begum	Respect	668
Muzibul Islam	Respect	498
Dave Anderson	BNP	358
Kevin Ovenden	Respect	277

Blackwall & Cubit Town		
Date	Electorate	Turnout (%)
22.5.2014	9193	31.64
Name	Party	Votes
Dave Chesterton	Lab	956
Christopher James Chapman	C	877
Candida Ronald	Lab	875
Anusur Rahman	Lab	872
Gloria Rose Thienel	C	815
Geeta Mohan Kasanga	C	762
Faruk Khan	THF	744
Kabir Ahmed	THF	726
Mohammed Aktaruzzaman	THF	713
Diane Lochner	UKIP	240
Paul Shea	UKIP	190
Anthony Registe	UKIP	188
Katy Guttman	G	110
Mark Lomas	G	98
Chris Smith	G	74
Elaine Bagshaw	L Dem	71
Richard Flowers	L Dem	68
Stephen Clarke	L Dem	58
Ellen Kenyon Peers	TUSC	11
John Peers	TUSC	11
Mohammed Akhlaqur Rahman	Ind	11

Whatever the phenomenon is, is there a pattern?

- Holy trinity x2
- St Dunstan's x2
- Millwall x2
- Limehouse
- Bow west
- Blackwall & Cubit town

It is clearly documented and backed by local knowledge that these wards were pre-dominantly made up of white British households. In all these cases it is the first time elections, and they are the common link, the second is that there was one Bangladeshi candidate with two white candidates. It seems to be the strategy to support getting the Bangladeshis elected in those white dominated areas in that era. The white elephant here is the racial element of the electorates.

Exclusivity

Labour party became exclusive and selective and not everyone could obtain membership for various reasons, and those that did become party members were able to form "a form of authority" within their sub-group and allow and disallow aspiring councillors to join, based on their affiliation to community groups and family clans. It is not possible to substantiate with evidence but are anecdotal, we can also take note that after 2 elections, nearly all Labour party members, then the third election 1990, you have Liberal Democrat candidates. This would have split the Bangladeshi community and a lot of heavy duty campaigning would have taken place for the Lib Dem candidates, the past decades of mistreat by the Lib Dem council leadership would not have been easily forgotten; however, these candidates did win and became members of the leadership group in the borough.

Natural Choice of the community

The natural selection and choice for the Bangladeshi community was Labour and those that had moved up economically, now chose Conservative. Even back then, it was the individuals who chose Liberal were able to further their political aspirations of becoming a councillor. Many of the community vanguards were in the forefront and with the Labour party, who were younger and more proficient in English.

Party Politics

The parties had recognised the dynamics by the third election term and realised their survival, especially the Liberal Democrats. They were putting up candidates for election. In 1990 they had their first Bangladeshi councillors but never over took Labour.

The community suffered in the 80's under the Liberal council and the community have not forgotten that, today it is difficult to get a Bengali Liberal democrat elected. The policy and the party does not appeal to the mass, however, there are a particular groups of Bangladeshis taking up the Liberal party line, it is noteworthy that many are not of Sylheti background.

Liberals & Liberal Democrats

It goes without saying, that the Bangladeshi community suffered under the Liberals and Liberal Democrats and they were the nemesis of the community. I remember the indignity we use to suffer, I'd pop in to the one stop shop and we would have to wait, or residents who did not speak English fluently had to take someone with them to explain and communicate and so on and more. The newer better quality housing were offered more to the Caucasian community than ours, and even when we were offered decent homes, the racists would force us out, only to be rehoused within the Bangladeshi community. So when a pompous ignoramus spurts out the words 'integration' remind them of their delusional past and even the current prejudices flourishing within Downing Street.

This is the reason why the party was despised and no community activists would choose to be with the liberals. However, this clearly wasn't the case; we did end up having Bangladeshi candidates who went on to become elected councillors; Sajjad Miah, Abdul Rohim, and Akikur Rahman to name the first few. Their length of service were numbered, and political carrers cut short, once the wider Bangladeshis got to grips with party politics. The Liberal Democrats hold in Tower Hamlets was over taken by Labour.

Why did the Bangladeshi persons choose to join the Liberal/Liberal Democrat party? It appears that all other parties were full to the ream with members, and opportunities were very slim. Joining the Lib Dem was one of the options to resort to, the other was independent, and independent without the community support was futile.

A twin pronged approach and resolve in the Bangladeshis infiltration of the Liberal Democrats. It was to be used for multitude of changes, make it Bangladeshi friendly, to educate them and soften their stance on the community, make it inclusive, give it a voice, an advocate, representative, influencer and so on.

The party was to engage with the community, work with those who were willing to. The party was also levelling themselves up with their competition - the Labour party. They would have had to adapt to the climate change of the borough in order to survive.

Conservative

The Conservative party in Tower Hamlets within the Bangladeshi community is still many decades behind. However, many of the business people in the community have reached a point in their success that they align themselves with the Conservative Party.

Many Bangladeshi individuals have stood for Conservatives in strong Labour wards and have failed to get elected. It is pointless to have a Bengali Conservative candidate in Spitalfields as it is still a ward where people are unemployed and reliant on welfare benefits, and have not been able to move up the economic ladder.

However, the Bangladeshi had their first councillors in the most unexpected ward. In 2010, it was the Millwall ward, Md Maium Miah won with 2519 votes. This is a first, he came third in the conservative group, this has become a pattern, of the Bengali councillors wining in Millwall.

Labour Party glory days

By 1994 the community had seen the changes it had achieved, and it seems that the motto of the community was, to an extent, that no Bangladeshi candidate other than Labour would be elected.

There were no Bangladeshi Liberal councillors until 2002. The borough and the Bangladeshi community soldiered on with the Labour party. From 1994 onwards the community had risen from obscurity and near death, after the attack on Quddus Ali. The community was awakened by the beatings subjected on Quddus Ali, all energies and resources were committed by the community leaders and activists and a political war was being fought and they were not taking any prisoners.

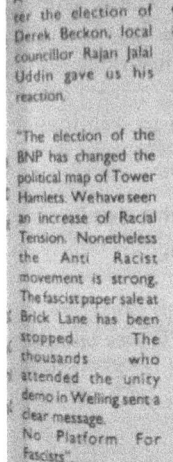
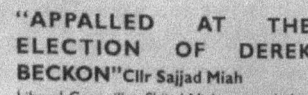

This is an article from the public informer and notes views of both parties. Cllr Jalal Uddin Labour & late Cllr Sajjad Miah Liberal Democrat.

The community strategy was one natural choice, and that was the Labour party, and majority of the Bangladeshi people along with all the supporters were out ensuring that racism is voted out. There was no room for the liberals and no Bangladeshi Liberal candidates won for the next two terms until 2002.

Ironically, it took killings and a beatings to acknowledge the successes of the Bangladeshi community in Tower Hamlets.

Reading Cllr Sajjad's statement, little did he know then, he was right, that by the next election, the Bangladeshi community did get rid of the BNP as well as him and all his Liberal Bangladeshi colleagues. The Bangladeshis were not in an open mood to receive Cllr Sajjad's comments about "However, we should allow Beackon to participate in the meetings, as he is elected representative" quite clearly while others did not recognise the BNP's win, cllr Sajjad Miah did in this article.

Political Playing Field Is Changing

Tower Hamlets is changing in many ways and the Bangladeshi dominance will subside.

Many Bangladeshis have moved out of Tower Hamlets, leaving behind their humble beginnings. It is like the natural progression from council estates to home ownership in other boroughs. Although many still own their Labour run ex-council properties. Many Bangladeshis thought their economical growth was through the Labour party, when in fact it was the Conservatives under Margeret Thatcher that empowered them through the right-to-buy. The families joining the single men in the 1960/70's was a result of the Labour governments policies, in particular putting a stop in sending of the remittance to their families back home.

The property prices booming out of control, has put a halt in this exodus and buying one to live in, is near impossible for the British Bangladeshi family in the current property market.

There has been an influx of a different ethnic minority within Tower Hamlets namely the Somali community and the North African community along with Eastern Europeans and the Italian non Sylheti community.

There is a growth in the Conservative party and in the Liberal party with non Sylhetis - diehard wanaby politicians.

STATEMENT OF PERSONS NOMINATED

London Borough of Tower Hamlets

Election of a Mayor of Tower Hamlets

The following is a statement of the persons nominated for election as a Mayor for

London Borough of Tower Hamlets

Name of Candidate	Home Address	Description (if any)	Name of Proposer	Reason why no longer nominated*
BAGSHAW Elaine	Flat 309 Pasmore Court, 26 New Festival Avenue, London, E14 6FW	Liberal Democrats	Clarke Stephen	
BIGGS John	Flat 30, Stepney City Apartments, 49 Clark Street, London, E1 3HS	Labour Party	Islam Sirajul	
ERLAM Andy	2 Joshua Pedley Mews, Bow, London, E3 2ZE	Red Flag - Anti-Corruption	Townsend Christine E.	
FOSTER John	11B Silvester House, Sceptre Road, London, E2 0JT	Green Party	Hancocks Benjamin E.	
GOLDS Peter	112 Langbourne Place, London, E14 3WW	The Conservative Party Candidate	King Neil A.	
HUDSON Vanessa Helen	Flat 2 Dusere House, 14 Viaduct Street, London, E2 0BZ	Animal Welfare Party	Todd Stephen R.	
KADIR Hafiz Abdul	25 Vallance Road, London, E1 5HS	Independent	Hoque Md Abdul	
KHAN Rabina	35 Callaghan Cottages, Lindley Street, London, E1 3AZ	Independent	Islam Syed F	
MCQUEEN Nicholas	1C Albert Gardens, London, E1 0LH	UK Independence Party (UKIP)	Webber Mark A.	
RAHMAN NANU Md Motiur	450 Cable Street, London, E1W 3DR	Independent	Begum Asma	

*Decision of the Returning Officer that the nomination is invalid or other reason why a person nominated no longer stands nominated

The persons above against whose name no entry is made in the last column have been and stand validly nominated

A POLL WILL BE TAKEN on Thursday 11 June 2015 between the hours of 7:00 am and 10:00 pm.
Where contested this poll is taken together with the election of a Borough Councillor

Dated: Friday 15 May 2015

John S. Williams
Returning Officer

Printed and published by the Returning Officer, Town Hall, 7th Floor, Mulberry Place, 5 Clove Crescent, London, E14 2BG

The community has also detached themselves from the major political parties and have established their own, such as the Respect party, Tower Hamlets First and now Peoples' Action Tower Hamlets group and as always independent.

Political participation is in the DNA of the Bangladeshis and as long as there is a large Bangladeshi community in Tower Hamlets they will be in local politics. There is evidence of gentrification all over the borough, where there are more white European residents in rented accommodations who have the white votes.

Shoreditch, Boundary Estate, Millwall, Canary Wharf and other areas are evident of the changes in voting and elected parties. Canary Wharf is Conservative stronghold and there are Liberal gains too.

Having collated the data it is clear where the shakers and movers are in the borough and how the boundary changes have helped.

We have two Somali Councillors and this community's aspirations will grow, just as the Bengali's did, and we might end up competing over our place.

It is clear from what happened over Mayor Lutfur Rahman, the commissioner coming in and installing a white person, John Biggs and then to clear up the council of any signs of the ex-mayor. It is possible that the powers that be will not allow the council to become 100% non white, however it is always healthy to keep a balance, no doubt.

Party Forming

Since the confidence of the community to form their own political groups, lead by the RESPECT party, has given us a different and very 'local' parties such as the THF & TPP and more.

Of the newly formed parties after RESPECT, THF did well to have 18 candidates out of 39 to be elected. This would have been a moral boost for them at the time. However, TPP has not done well, and it will be safe to say that this knowhow of forming political parties does not automatically mean success.

This is where the growth of the community can be seen clearly, when the people are establishing new groups to take position in the community. This process requires leaders, people who will follow, administration, financers, a lot of backing from the community.

(The following articles were compiled from the Love Wapping site, www.lovewapping.org)

Following parties have been formed

Tower Hamlets First (THF)
Tower Hamlets First was a British political party represented in Tower Hamlets London Borough Council, which was launched to contest the 2014 local elections in the Borough. During its existence it was the second largest party in Tower Hamlets Council and the fifth largest political party out of all London borough councils.

Tower Hamlets First was established by Lutfur Rahman on 18 September 2013. The party stood candidates in the 2014 Tower Hamlets Council election,[2][3] where it won 18 out of 45 seats, becoming the second largest party on Tower Hamlets Council, and the fifth largest political party out of all London borough councils.

Nick Cohen in The Guardian described the party as a cult of personality surrounding Lutfur Rahman.[4] The party was suspended in 23 April 2015, after an Election Court report that found Rahman "personally guilty of 'corrupt or illegal practices' or both" with the party labelled as a "one-man band". The party was removed from the list of political parties maintained by the Electoral Commission on 29 April 2015.

People's Alliance Tower Hamlets (PATH)

Rabina Khan's road from THING to PATH

Rabina Khan, Cabinet Member for Housing in the Rahman administration, ran against Labour's John Biggs in the court ordered rerun of the rigged 2014 Mayoral election and did very well indeed with over 26,000 votes against the nearly 33,000 for Biggs after the second preference and final count.

Khan is regarded as one of the most able street politicians in the Borough although not so competent in the Council chamber and has yet to show clear water between herself and the corruption of Lutfur Rahman.

She was one of the Tower Hamlets First councillors deemed elected 'with the benefit of corrupt and illegal practices' by Justice Mawrey but have remained in their positions ever since.

Since 2014 Rahman's Tower Hamlets First party has morphed into the loose alliance known as the Tower Hamlets Independent Group (aka THING) and another group led by Cllr Rabina Khan (Shadwell People's Alliance of Tower Hamlets).

In November 2016 Rabina and her husband, Islamic Forum Europe stalwart Aminur Khan, quit THING and formed the People's Alliance of Tower Hamlets (PATH) . Current members of PATH are:

- *Rabina Khan (Shadwell People's Alliance of Tower Hamlets)*
- *Shafi Ahmed (Whitechapel People's Alliance of Tower Hamlets)*
- *Shah Alam (Mile End People's Alliance of Tower Hamlets)*
- *Abdul Asad (Shadwell People's Alliance of Tower Hamlets)*
- *Aminur Khan (Shadwell People's Alliance of Tower Hamlets)*

Who are 'Tower Hamlets Together'?(THT)
The only documentation on the Electoral Commission site relating to the Tower Hamlets Together application.

The Wapping Mole discovered the existence of the application by 'Tower Hamlets First' ' Tower Hamlets Together' (above) submitted on 23rd December 2016 to become a registered political party by pure chance despite the incredibly bad functionality of the Electoral Commission site.

(The Electoral Commission site is not fit for purpose as it makes it more difficult to undertake basic research into UK political parties, not easier. As such it is a fundamental obstacle for anyone wishing to find out about political developments in Tower Hamlets or any other part of the country.

But then as the events of the last few years in Tower Hamlets have demonstrated the Electoral Commission itself is not fit for purpose, so at least its website is consistent with its real world activities.)

Some clues as to the heritage of THT can be gleaned from the proposed logo of THT and the logo of Tower Hamlets First.

Tower Hamlets Together logo   Tower Hamlets First logo

Compare and contrast. Tower Hamlets Together logo and the Tower Hamlets First logo.
Can you spot the difference? Answers on a postcard please (or a tweet).

A spokesperson for the Electoral Commission was unable to provide LW with any details of the people or organisations who have submitted the 'Tower Hamlets Together' application but said: "If the application contains all of the correct information, we aim to let the applicant know the result of their application *within 30 working days of receipt of a completed application. The guidance also states that we don't make the details of party officers public until the party has been registered. At that point the names of the officers and the address of their party headquarters is made available on our website."*

The Electoral Commission application also details proposed descriptions for Tower Hamlets First as:

1. Tower Hamlets Together
2. Bringing Tower Hamlets Together
3. Stronger Together
4. Better Together
5. We can together

The alternative descriptions may well be the subject of a future LW alternative logo competition for Tower Hamlets Together.

Tower Hamlets residents need not be rocket scientists or brain surgeons to work out that 'Tower Hamlets Together' is almost certainly going to consist of the current Tower Hamlets Independent Group of councillors as listed below:

Cllr. Ohid Ahmed (Lansbury Independent Group)
Cllr. Sulu Ahmed (Spitalfields & Banglatown Independent Group)
Cllr. Mahbub Alam (St. Dunstan's Independent Group)
Cllr. Gullam Kabria Choudhury (Poplar Independent Group)
Cllr. Harun Miah (Shadwell Independent Group)
Cllr. Md. Maium Miah (Canary Wharf Independent Group)
Cllr. Muhammad Ansar Mustaquim (St Peter's Independent Group)
Cllr. Oliur Rahman (Stepney Green Independent Group)
Cllr. Gulam Robbani (Spitalfields & Banglatown Independent Group)
You can view all the different political parties in Tower Hamlets on the Council website although this is subject to change, sometimes on a minute by minute basis.

(These articles were compiled from the Love Wapping site, www.lovewapping.org)

This is a site where the local councillors are scrutinesed and held accounted and accountable, something the Bangladeshi community is incapable of doing.

We witness here the recording of the growth in the local political arenaby independent entities. A lot can be said and made about the "shifts at will", of the independent votes. This must have been alarming to the establishment, hitting the heart of British politics. If they can do it, so can others, and sure enough we did see it, the Brexit party being one of them.
Now, the rise of independent councillors is a worrying matter for the main parties. These individuals win, they have the voters, and those that vote for them do not vote for any of the main parties.These voters were not any main party loyalists, they're floaters or rather, led by the cause of that moment in time. In the political world, this must be a reality call.

This was a unique opportunity for the British Bangladeshi politicians to take advantage of, the borough could have its own political group soley determined by the Bangladeshi vote, and it is still possible.

However, there are those die hard Labour members, and now the Labour borough council has made it possible so that counncillors can make a living out of being a councillor, as the allowances have become similar to a basic salary. This has allowed the less employable due to their ageto live with a decent allowance which is attached to the councillor position. All are happy and there is no dissent, or reduction in the vote outage or leaks through the councillors on the payroll.

Incidently the rate of allowance increase started from Lutfur Rahman's era but then John Biggs capitalised on it.

Party Hopping

Data shows individuals have hopped parties in order to win an election or changed the party after they got elected.

In the early years some of the community members went in as independent due to issues regarding membership to political parties. In subsequent elections individuals either joined parties or were head hunted by them.

As the community grew in politics, party politics and the knowhow, the councillors and community groups started forming their own parties, such as Respect, Tower Hamlets First and People's Alliance Tower Hamlets.

We can see many have party hopped, the hopping is often self explanatory based on the timing of a particular hop.

Party hopping soon after being elected - candidates that campaign as an independent or an affiliate of a party, change party soon after being elected. All this is very dubious to the eye of the electorate which leaves the younger generation further disenfranchised with politics and its processes. This in itself is an act of "selling out," having promised to represent their voters with what they sold them, and then to get in and change into another parties colour – "cloak and dagger."

The definition of a selling out in this book is that of "those who campaign with one group and then change soon after being elected and enter into the council chambers." Those that hop parties after serving their term are not viewed in this book as "selling out their soul," more of selling their political standing. Candidates are free to change their mind to what they believe in, or be influenced by well spoken and presented leaders.

It is also the case after having spoken to a few councillors that it is all about party politics and an individual/independent councillor doesn't have much clout or power, nor control, and will most certainly be drowned out to enforce or influence any change. The prospect they face upon entering the chambers is one of being touted to change, join the majority group or the party that has a national standing.

Then there are those that have hopped party where there is a greater chance of winning. Then there are those that have hopped party because it serves their beliefs and morals.

Break down of the votes

Many Bangladeshi voters have enjoyed their successes, some of the prominent individuals who have won more than their fair share, owe it to their voters.

As a party member and a party candidate they benefited from those secure votes. The party members and the general public who support the national party.

Individually, they would have relied on their friends and family, immediate and extended and then those of the same village, same ward and district.

They would have also benefited from the same cultural, religious and political affiliated background.

And finally those who they have won over with their manifesto and charm.

Family: That naturally goes without saying that all members of the family will be supporting and voting for them as it is a matter of prestige. This will be received and appreciated well "back home" in Bangladesh. It will hold a significant position in Bangladesh, in their village and ward, where they will get recognition as a dignitary or as a VIP and be respected.

Friends: It also goes without saying that they will support them as this is something the candidate will remember and recognise, these friends will want respect back, by way of feeling proud that they are associated with the candidate and pride themselves of the respect that comes with it.

Extended family: They will also be canvassed and secure their support and votes. They will then support the candidate by passing on word of mouth to other relations; this then will extend to others from the same and enamouring **villages** who live in the borough, ward.

Village and district: The candidate reaching out beyond their ancestral village, to that of their entire district, either here or in Bangladesh. Word will get around that so and so has stood as a candidate.

Cultural affiliation, whether they are singers, dancers, land owners, business owner, this will also touch a note with the culture votes; moving on to the religious votes. There are two main grouping in this section, the Sufis and the Jamati's, the remnants of Abu Ala Maududi's teachings. Sufi is the original strain/sect of Islam practiced in the land of Bangladesh and in particular the Sylhet region; this is the sect of muslims in the Brick Lane Mosque and all mosque which bares the name of Shah Jalal, Shah Poran (Forhan) and Burhan, these are the Sufi saints of Sylhet District and there are many more dotted around Bangladesh.

Then you have the sect borne out of rebellion, to reach the steps of power by any means necessary, the over throwing of power, legitimising revolution, origins of which are in Europe.

This is another area where votes are secured based on their religious affiliation. Much of the religious votes will be made up by their family members and the extended members, the significance here is capturing the non-family members.

While we can go on dissecting the votes, the point that needs to be noted is the vote of the youth, those that are 18-24, male and female. That is part and parcel of the canvassing of the family voters along with canvassing with the community organisations and charities promoting their manifestos. Benefiting friends who support the contestant and are part of the network.

Lastly the gender vote, in particular the female votes canvassed with the help of female family members while males canvassing on your behalf with males.

Having noted the above, it will be correct to state that this is very subjective and is a generalised opinion, when it comes to canvassing for votes one thing can be said for sure is that creativeness and pragmatism goes in all directions to win and election.

Manifesto: this is the sales product that will attract the no nonsense voters who have no affiliation at all with the candidate. Their manifesto will appeal to them and will vote accordingly.

It is the general information to the community at large and this portion is divided so thinly because of the increased rate of Bangladeshi candidates. This is possibly a political tactic played by the parties.

Allowances

Allowance has always been there for councillors so it is nothing new. In recent times the allowance has gone up and councillors can make a decent income from attending these meetings as well as taking on cabinet roles.

Role	Independent Review 2014 * (£)	Current Tower Hamlets amended Member Allowance Scheme	Proposed Tower Hamlets amended Member Allowance Scheme 2016/17
Basic Allowance	10938	10390	10938
Mayor	83639	67094	75000
Statutory Deputy Mayor	35900-42591	15217	16000
Leader of the Majority Group on the Council	15826-29209	13065	11300
Leader of the largest Opposition Group	15826-29209	10502	11300
Leader of any Group (subject to having at least 10% of the Council)	2444-9137	5709	8000
Cabinet Members	35900-42591	13065	14000
Mayoral Adviser	2444-9137	-	7000
Chair of Overview and Scrutiny Committee	35900-42591	10502	11000
Chair of Scrutiny Sub-Committee	15826-29209	7801	8000
Chair of Development Committee	15826-29209	10502	11000
Chair of Licensing	15826-29209	7801	6000
Chair of General Purposes Committee	2444-9137	7801	8000
Chair of Audit Committee	2444-9137	5709	6000
Chair of Pensions Committee	2444-9137	5709	6000
Speaker	-	-	7801
Deputy Speaker	-	-	3899

Current SRA title	Current SRA level	New SRA title	New SRA£	Change from current	2018 Independent Panel Recommendation
Elected Mayor	£75,000.00	Elected Mayor	£ 75,000.00	Unchanged	£85,162
Deputy Mayor Statutory	£16,000.00	Deputy Mayor (x3)	£ 30,000.00	£ 14,000.00	£36,917 to £43,060 (deputy leader of the council)
SRA Leader of the Opposition	£11,300.00	SRA Leader of the Opposition (subject to having at least 10% of the Council)	£ 11,300.00	and not be taken up following election	£16,227 to £29,797 (Leader of principal opposition group)
		SRA Leader of the Opposition (if Group has fewer than 10% of the Council)	£ 5,000.00	New SRA	
Cabinet Member (x8)	£14,000.00	Cabinet member (x8)	£ 20,000.00	£ 6,000.00	£36,917 to £85,460
		Chief Whip	£ 11,000.00	New SRA	£16,227 to £29,797 (majority party whip)

Title	Number	Current	Proposed	Increase	Total Increase PA	Total Cost PA
Mayor	1	£75,000	£75,000	£0	£0	£75,000
Statutory Deputy Mayor	1	£16,000	£30,000	£14,000	£14,000	£30,000
Deputy Mayor	2	£16,000	£30,000	£14,000	£28,000	£60,000
Leader of any Opposition Group *	1	£0	£5,000	£5,000	£5,000	£5,000
Cabinet Member	8	£14,000	£20,000	£6,000	£48,000	£160,000
Chief Whip	1	£0	£11,000	£11,000	£11,000	£11,000
Mayoral Advisors	3	£7,000	£12,000	£5,000	£15,000	£36,000
* Having less than 10% of total Council					£121,000	£377,000

LONDON BOROUGH OF TOWER HAMLETS

MEMBERS' ALLOWANCE SCHEME 2013/2014

Notice is hereby given under the provisions of the Local Authorities (Members Allowances) (England) Regulations, 2003, of the payment, for the financial year 2013/2014, of the following allowances to Council Members.

Councillor	Basic Allowance	Special Responsibility Allowance	Travelling and subsistence allowance	Dependants' carers allowance	TOTAL
H U ABBAS	10,166.04	10,275.72			£20,441.76
A M O AHMED	10,166.04	14,889.48			£25,055.52
K AHMED	10,166.04				£10,166.04
K U AHMED	10,166.04				£10,166.04
R AHMED	10,166.04	1,056.35			£11,222.39
R U AHMED	10,166.04	12,784.56			£22,950.60
S. ALI	10,166.04	12,784.56			£22,950.60
T J ARCHER	10,166.04	1,076.67			£11,242.71
A ASAD	10,166.04	12,784.56			£22,950.60
C ASTON	10,166.04				£10,166.04
L BEGUM	10,166.04				£10,166.04
M R CHAUDHURY	10,166.04	4805.37			£14,971.41
A CHOUDHURY	10,166.04	12,784.56			£22,950.60
Z DAVIS	10,166.04				£10,166.04
S EATON	10,166.04	7,632.60			£17,798.64
D EDGAR	10,166.04				£10,166.04
M FRANCIS	10,166.04				£10,166.04
J GARDNER	10,166.04				£10,166.04
C GIBBS	10,166.04	5,586.24			£15,752.28
P. GOLDS	10,166.04	10,275.72			£20,441.76
S. HAQUE	10,166.04	12,784.56			£22,950.60
C HARPER-PENMAN	10,166.04	7632.60			£17,798.64
S. ISLAM	10,166.04	12,258.28			£22,424.32
A JACKSON	10,166.04	1,422.17			£11,588.21
D JONES	10,166.04				£10,166.04
E L JONES	10,166.04				£10,166.04
RANIA KHAN	10,166.04	12,784.56			£22,950.60
A R KHAN	10,166.04				£10,166.04
A KHAN	10,166.04				£10,166.04
R KHAN	10,166.04	12,784.56		7,180.18	£30,130.78
S. KHATUN	10,166.04	7,632.60			£17,798.64
H MIAH	10,166.04				£10,166.04
M M MIAH	10,166.04				£10,166.04
F MIAH	10,166.04				£10,166.04
M. MUKIT	10,166.04	4,062.42			£14,228.46
A OMER	10,166.04				£10,166.04
L PAVITT	10,166.04	7,098.93			£17,264.97
J PECK	10,166.04	884.70			£11,050.74
J PIERCE	10,166.04				£10,166.04
L RAHMAN	85,649.96				£85,649.96
O. RAHMAN	10,166.04	12,784.56			£22,950.60
Z RAHMAN	10,166.04	5,586.24			£15,752.28
G. ROBBANI	10,166.04				£10,166.04
R SAUNDERS	10,166.04	7,632.60			£17,798.64
O A SNOWDON	10,166.04	6,296.90			£16,462.94
G R THIENEL	10,166.04				£10,166.04
B. TURNER	10,166.04	7,632.60			£17,798.64
H UDDIN	10,166.04	7,632.60			£17,798.64
K UDDIN	10,166.04				£10,166.04
A ULLAH	10,166.04	6,296.90			£16,462.94
M UZ-ZAMAN	10,166.04	9,732.87			£19,898.91
A L WHITELOCK	10,166.04	7,632.60			£17,798.64
TOTAL	**584,118.00**	**257,309.64**		**7,180.18**	**848,607.82**

It is clear from the rate of allowance given to each councillor that it is as good as a part time job. It is even better if you have a significant role, such as a cabinet member, then it is equivalent to a full time job.

So taking on the role of a councillor is rewarding financially, a councillor has potential to get allowance of up to £30,000.00, and with speakers responsibility £40,000.00.

Clearly things have moved on since the days of Md Ashik Ali and Md Nurul Huque from 1982, the allowances are better than the Zero hour contracts.

It is clear to see why some people have made it their career to be a councillor. The qualification required for this post is life experience, intelligence, you don't need a degree, nor do you need to have good reading or writing skills. You just need to have a burning desire to benefit your community/locality. The people do the rest, they vote you in. Once you are in, then you are in a different league, level, the council chamber does not belong to any party and the council employees dance to the tune of those elected in.

From the 2013/14 Allowance list we can see who earned how much.

Following councillors took home over £20k+, this is equivenlent of a Salary:

1. L. Rahman — £85k+
2. R. Khan — £30k+
3. A. M. O. Ahmed — £25k+
4. R. U. Ahmed — £22k+
5. S. Ali — £22k+
6. A. Asad — £22k+
7. A. Chaudhury — £22k+
8. S. Haque — £22k+
9. S. Islam — £22k+
10. Rania Khan — £22k+
11. O. Rahman — £22k+
12. H. U. Abbas — £20k+

Taking on cabinet roles boosts the basic allowance, so, for many people it becomes a means of employment. We also need get value for money

Aptitude

A Bangladeshi councillor explained the aptitude required to do this job. It is the responsibility of the councillors to hold their departments to account, for example those in the position of dealing with money.

Whoever is responsible for overseeing it needs to scrutinise the accounts and have the ability to ensure value for money is always achieved or attained. Hold individuals to account as well as support for any eventualities.

Many councillors according to ex-councillors are "yes sirs", they will agree to everything, useful instruments to the parties. Similarly the "boot & ass lickers," they do the same; in doing this ensure longevity and benefits.

Over time the council has seen many strong educated candidates and one being Lutfur Rahman, who then was targeted and nationally disgraced. This is now slowly falling away as he is now being found not guilty as the spun conspiracy unravels itself.

The community's senior generation, while enigmatic and have the charisma with the Bangladeshi community in spoken Bengali, it is a daunting dynamic for them to speak and have conversations and debates in English. Articulate themselves in the public arena, formal and informal.

There were many Bangladeshi councillors who were not able to articulate themselves, like Councillor Selim Ullah, Gulam Mortuzza and others who did well to educate and better themselves to meet the demands of their roles.

It is clear that spoken English was an issue with majority of the first generation Bangladeshi community young and old. Many of the first generation youth lacked confidence due to being ridiculed in class and receiving a battering outside by racists. This heavily contributed to the poor attainment of a formal education. This created an opportunity for the educated or the senior community 'vanguards' to ultimately create an exclusive club.

Discontent

There have been many rifts within the community and between individuals, with recriminations from past and present councillors. There are many terms used now to describe the councillors;

"Yes sirs"
"Boot lickers"
"Ass lickers"

This political journey comes at a cost, not cheap and easy, some have been accused of selling themselves, their values, integrity, and even the community.

It is no secret that many of the Bangladeshi councillors were not Oxford or Cambridge University educated and thus lack many attributes of being educated, although generally not all politicians are educated to university level.

However, many have remained in politics and many have not. Many strong councillors had a short career without having to sell their integrity. Many of those capable of challenging and scrutinising have been systematically ousted.

Once the councillors are elected, they have to tag the party line and are led by the whip. The party members are required to adhere to the whip otherwise they are not part of the team. This inevitably compromises their ideals and what they stood for, which got them the votes in the first place.

There was a growing enmity between individuals, growing rivalries and of course "divide and rule" was at play, it was the natural order of play, when there is strength and unity.

Bad Press

The following images are a collection of what the media had to say about the issues arising out of the Bangladeshi councillors. They all highlight some cultural aspects of the community, however, when the national papers get hold of it, it is sensationalised.

	London Evening Standards Coverage		
	Local media coverage		Telegraph coverage
	BBC News Coverage		The Guardian Coverage
	The Evening Standards coverage		The Guardian coverage on-line

It was inevitable that the community was going to reach these points as the role was significant and the people were learners of the industry. The process was shaping the quality and standards in all walks of life, it is a step outside of the Bangladeshi politics and the accountability is commanded.

The process is educating the mass Bangladeshis who want a piece of this cake, that its accessible to all. These accountability results woke people up to understand what is demanded of them as councillors. It lets the wannabe councillors know that it is the British way, it is subjective and individuals today come with a wealth of public relations skills and creativity.

Some individuals have had a wake-up call, the Bangladeshi way will only take you so far and others have fallen prey to individual's wrath.

It was only a matter of time before daggers were wielded in public, the take down of the first elected Mayor of Tower Hamlets Lutfur Rahman, was initiated by a Bangladeshi. Maybe decades from now we will learn of the winners and lossers, that is another book for another time.

The community was in the "limelight", and this was at the centre many of whom failed to fathom, over time it would only create resentments and schemes to dim the light. There is so much infighting among Bangladeshi politicians, that it would be easy for outsiders to apply the colonial "divide and rule" ointment.

These bad presses have catapulted the Bangladeshi community from local news to national and international. We've seen it in movies, when the authorities want to take a person down, they discredit the individual and dig up all the trash to reduce the person to the point of shame and so on.

> "What a way for Lutfur Rahman ex mayor to make his mark, he stamped his achievement in British and Tower Hamlets history and his demise too. History will judge him".

And in the meantime the local and national media have put the Tower Hamlets's councillor to scrutiny. We also have "LoveWapping" and "Trial by Jeory," who are the local scrutinisers; they hold them accountable for their actions. They are riveting to read as their subject is dissected and held to account. It is not always clear as to their motives when they are hounded by the two scrutinisers. Maybe clarifying the intent, the aims and objectives will lead to a more widely received audience rather then seeming like a witch hunt.

There are positivities coming out of these bad press, the community is opening their eyes, realising their role and position in British society, they are recognising the values of the country they live in and how much they want to distance themselves from many of the traditional Bangladeshi ways; the current high tech generation is alien to the Bangladeshi rural traditions and customs with varying strands based on ancestral region, this however is a generalisation.

2010

2010 election was a combination of sheer effort and dedication with well thought through strategies. The groups, the manpower and the hours put in was nothing compared to the cost to everyone in the community.

> *"That, elusive parliament member that, we have not, yet secured."*

This was about to change and the build up to the election had everyone in a frenzy so much was pinned on it. It was time to put forward the candidates for the MP-ship and this time a definate winning Bangladeshi MP.

Based on the roles Rushanara had leading up to the election, these various roles and positions, meant that she looked very much the winning candidate.

The in-fighting had ensued with the community and amongst the male population, and as always a few put themselves forward, election politics, strategies to manipulate the results and out comes. Many unsuitable candidates are fielded to split the votes; the more candidates there are the further the reduction of votes.

This can be mapped in the tables included in the appendice. 2010 was a double wammy, the elected mayoral campaign was underway and the contests was between two Bangladeshi rivals of similar peerage; Helal Uddin Abbas & Lutfur Rahman. So this was a dead cert that a Bangladesh mayor will be hailed.

Yet, not so confident from the public setting regarding the parliamentary election as there were a few people who were charismatic in the community.

In both the election settings, by the time the election was due; we the residents had already been part of the political show of hustlings and campaignings for over a year. The coming elections were ear marked for the Sylheti community.

The "will of the people" was like a heavy duvet over the borough, it was happening; it wasn't a matter of when and who any more; Bangladeshi MP and Mayor was confirmed and won in principle. So leading up to the election, it was more of a case of, which Bangladeshi to vote for.

So going into the election was a win win situation. The consequences of which was that the community was split, there was a fraction. The community could not enjoy the harmonious, joyous moment for the whole community of the borough and rest of the country. Yet again, planting of division, and evidently the divisions then also brought down the Bangladeshi Mayorship.

Tower Hamlets Bethnal Green & Bow		
Year	Electorate	Turnout (%)
2005	82,599	53.3
Name	Party	Votes
G. Galloway	RU	15801
Miss O.T. King	Lab	14978
S. Bahkt Faruk	C	6244
Syed Nurul Islam Dulu	L Dem	4928
J.P.W Foster	GP	1950
E. Etefia	Ind	68
Miss C. Pugh	CL	38

Tower Hamlets Bethnal Green & Bow		
Year	Electorate	Turnout (%)
2010	81,243	63.25
Name	Party	Votes
Rushanara Ali	Lab	21784
Ajmal Masroor	L Dem	10210
Abjol Miah	Res	8532
Zakir Hussain Khan	C	7071
Jeffrey Christpher Marshall	BNP	1405
Farid Bakth	G	856
Patrick Brooks	Ind	277
Alexander Rene Van-Terheyden	Ind	213
Hasib Hikmat	Ind	209
Mahmood Choudhury	Ind	100
Ahmed Abdul Malik	Ind	71

The above two tables indicate the number of individuals standing for election. In 2010 we had 11 candidates standing out of which 8 candidates were Bangladeshi.

There is much to be read in to the 2010 table. The list of names of candidates; indirectly and unofficially signed and sealed a Bangladeshi MP. Also to note that this opportunity also gives other unseasoned candidates to get a ride on this historical moment in Bangladeshi, Sylheti feat etched into British history.

If there were fewer candidates then Rushanara would have won by thousands of more votes. We can see, even though Rushanara was the favourite, she did not get a easy passage, the main three Bangaldeshi male candidates meant business.They were not to be looked down upon like pittance, they had a serious following; the other groups certainly had their strategies to attack the labour vote.There were nuances that could be drawn out of these results, the labour votes for Rushanara meant more of a liberal vote from the Bangladeshi voter. It is my opinion that the three Bangladeshi male candidates received the more preservative religious base votes; the Conservative party also benefiting from that because of the candidate; as well as their non-muslim conservative votes. It goes without saying that there were so many things going on and playing out simultaneously. That is the way of the fractured political mindset of our community

The dirtiest and bloodiest fight was for the Mayorship in the Sylhety community of Tower Hamlets. The contest between Helal Uddin Abbas & Lutfur Rahman was fought on so many different levels, only a politician would fathom such lengths.

The Mayoral position wasn't part of the community's political aspirations, so when the position arose individuals begun to make their moves. They were both Labour party members and councillors but Lutfur Rahman fell out and out of rank.

Helal Uddin Abbas is a die-hard Labour party member - well that's from my own observations of his standing in the community, and where he spends his time and attention.

In the order of seniority in the political field, Helal Uddin Abbas was the senior, and in an ideal world he would have had an honourary transition to the post and role of seniority. However that was not the case clearly. This role was more powerfull locally than a member of parliament, with so many resources and the power it weilded within the borough.

What ensued will go down in history, the witch hunt and defaming, not just an individual in politics but as a son of Bangladesh, the one that represented all of the boroughs residents. We saw him transform what was left untouched and dilapidated by the formidable Labour government of Tony Blair, the Poplar Baths. One of the jewels of the borough left to rot until Lutfur Rahman begun the restorational works. So much occurred and shaped the elected mayor's role and life. He afterall inherited the wrath that followed and befelled him.

Political Pathfinders

While Helal Uddin Abbas remains in the public eye and life, Lutfur Rahman has a job to rebuild his life after the Government of the country took him out of office, through devised strategies.

88

Candidates per Party

This table shows how many Bangladeshi candidates were per party over the period 1982-2016. This is to give an oversight

Party	Candidates	Elected
Conservatives	82	1
Green Party	2	0
Ind L Dem	1	0
Ind Lab	3	0
Independent	49	3
Labour	168	127
Liberal Democrats	92	11
Respect	72	14
Social Democratic Party (SDP)	8	0
The People's Party (TPP)	1	0
Tower Hamlets Community Campaign (CC)	4	0
Tower Hamlets First (THF)	39	18
Trade Union Solidarity Congress (TUSC)	1	0

This table paints a picture of how the placid community has become an active group of people on the political spectrum of the country and the parties.

The top six parties who have had the most candidates are:
1. Labour 168
2. Liberal Democrats 92
3. Conservatives 82
4. Respect 72
5. THF 39

Top four parties who had candidates elected are:
1. Labour 127
2. THF 18
3. Respect 14
4. Lib Dem 11

Over time it looks like Labour Party has redeemed them selves since, pre 1978 days.

Councillors: Per Election

Here the table shows how many councillors were elected and how many wards contested. It also breaks down the gender of the elected councillors.

Year	Females	Male	Wards Contested	Elected
1982	0	11	4	2
1985	0	2	1	1
1986	0	15	7	5
1988	0	1	1	0
1990	1	24	9	9
1992	0	1	1	1
1994	1	30	9	11
1995	0	3	2	2
1998	2	32	15	14
2001	0	1	1	1
2002	2	64	16	29
2006	13	91	15	31
2008	2	8	3	1
2010	17	112	17	29
2012	0	2	1	0
2014	10	68	19	26
2015	1	2	1	1
2016	0	1	1	1

The above table is a snap shot of the true meaning for the community. For the Sylhet community of Bangladesh that has changed the British & local political history, since the colonial times.

This is thepicture that paints a million words, of a nation borne out of oppression and injustice, a new nation of 1971 that has progressed in a relatively short national history and what lies ahead ofit.

How Many Councillors by Ward

Since the entrance of the Bangladeshi community in local elections the ward boundarieshave changed twice so far. The community started when the old boundaries were in place between 1978-1998, whichthen changed in 2002 and then again in 2014. It is facinating to see the results and you can immediately identify the communities strength and weaknesses.

These tables indicate how many councillors were elected in each of the wards per boundary changes since 1982.

1978-1998 Boundary (19 wards)

Wards	Councillors
Blackwall	1
Bow	0
Bromley	1
East India	0
Grove	0
Holy Trinity	2
Lansbury	0
Limehouse	3
Millwall	0
Park	0
Redcoat	1
Shadwell	5
Spitalfields	14
St Dunstan's	3
St Jame's	0
St Katharine's	9
St Mary's	1
St Peter's	3
Weavers	4

Tables in this section gives us an overview of the political shifts within the borough, through each boundary changes. Take note of the boundary manipulations that shapethe election results. Clear indication of the social think tank and its purposes.

The 19 ward boundries of 1987-1998 the community did well to get councillors elected in 12 wards but not in 7.

The seven wards that the community did not get any councillors in, were Bow, East India, Grove, lansbury, Millwall, Park and St Jame's.

The community did very well in Spitalfields 14 councillors, St Katharine's 9 councillors and Shadwell 5 councillors

2002-2010 Boundary (17 wards)

Wards	Councillors
Bethnal Green North	4
Bethnal Green South	7
Blackwall & Cubitt Town	1
Bow East	0
Bow West	2
Bromley by bow	8
East India & Lansbury	8
Limehouse	5
Mile End & Globe Town	4
Mile End East	7
Millwall	2
Shadwell	8
Spitalfields & Bangla Town	10
St Dunstan's & Stepney green	8
St Katharine's & Wapping	3
Weavers	5
Whitechapel	9

Then in 2002 the boundary was changed and the election dynamics changed. There were 2 less wards but the communities stronghold and weakhold had not changed. Spitafields remained the strong hold and Bow East remained the weakhold. Bow East covers the old Park ward.

In contrast the comunity did better because of the boundary change as it had councillors in 16 wards out of 17.

2014 -2016 Boundary (20 wards)

Wards	Councillors
Bethnal Green	2
Blackwall & Cubitt Town	0
Bomley South	1
Bow East	0
Bow West	1
Bromley North	2
Canary Wharf	1
Island Gardens	0
Lansbury	3
Limeouse	0
Mile End	1
Poplar	1
Shadwell	2
Spitalfields & Banglatown	2
St Dunstan's	2
St Katharine's & Wapping	0
St Peter's	2
Stepney Green	3
Weavers	1
Whitechapel	4

The third boundary change in 2014 saw an increase in the wards to 20, and the renaming of the wards, Milwall now became Canary Wharf, the ward that symbolised "white racist land" had now been swallowed up by the glitz of the Canary Wharf business zone.

If this is a permananet change then the history of Millwall is now left in the annals of history, it will no longer bring up spine chilling thoughts and experiences.

It is also note worthy that Bow East remains the same, the Bangladeshi community hasn't managed to get any councillors in that area, possibly due to the make up of community. This is an interesting point to note as it brings up the following question, are the councillors party lead, or community lead?

Reflecting on St Katharine's & Wapping ward, where the Bangladeshi councillorship begun with the election of Md Ashik Ali in 1982, fruits of which have been reaped since, and the point from where the roots flourished for the community to build their political foundation. We see a decline in the bangladeshi councillors,during the 2014 election there was no presence of a mainstream party representative contesting the seats other than theTower Hamlets First candidate, who came fifth. This will be the topic of the next book, exploring 35 years of politics for the Bangladeshi community in Tower Hamlets.

The First Councillors in each ward

This section you'll find a list of wards per boundary and their first elected Bangladeshi councillor.

The following tables paint a picture of the individual councillors and of the wards, for they are the pioneers who entered in to the ward politics which is intrinsically etched in to the political picture of the borough, the country and the parties.

1978-1998 Boundary (19 wards)

Wards	Councillors	Party	Date
Blackwall	Kumar Murshid	Lab	1998
Bow	Unsuccessful		
Bromley	Abdul Aziz Sardar	Lab	1998
East India	Unsuccessful		
Grove	Unsuccessful		
Holy Trinity	Akikur Rahman	LD	1990
Lansbury	Unsuccessful		
Limehouse	Soyful Alom	Lab	1994
Millwall	Unsuccessful		
Park	Unsuccessful		
Redcoat	Ataur Rahman	Lab	1998
Shadwell	Mrs Pola Uddin	Lab	1990
Spitalfields	Md Nurul Huque	Ind	1982
St Dunstan's	Jahangir Alam	Lab	1986
St Jame's	Unsuccessful		
St Katharine's	Md Asik Ali	Lab	1982
St Mary's	Bodrul Alom	Lab	1994
St Peter's	Abdul Rahim	LD	1990
Weavers	Sajjad Miah	LD	1990

In this period of 1978-1998, the community was successful in getting 12 wards out of 19, starting from 1982. Since then many other Bangladeshis contended in the wards, however, we respectfully give recognition of the pioneers that paved the way to leave their legacy.

2002-2010 Boundary (17 wards)

Wards	Councillors	Party	Date
Bethnal Green North	Azizur Rahman Khan	LD	2002
Bethnal Green South	Sirajul Islam/ Selim Ullah	Lab	2002
Blackwall & Cubitt Town	Lutfur Rahman Ali	Lab	2002
Bow East	Unsuccessful		
Bow West	Anwara Ali	Lab	2006
Bromley by bow	Abdul Aziz Sardar	Lab	2006
East India & Lansbury	Ohid Ahmed	Lab	2002
Limehouse	Soyful Alom	Lab	1994
Mile End & Globe Town	Md Jainal Uddin Choudhury	LD	2002
Mile End East	Helal Rahman	Lab	2002
Millwall	Mumtaz Samad	Lab	2002
Shadwell	Mrs Pola Uddin	Lab	1990
Spitalfields & Bangla Town	Helal Uddn Abbas	Lab	2002
St Dunstan's & Stepney Green	Ataur Rahman	Lab	2002
St Katharine's & Wapping	Shafiqul Haque	Lab	2002
Weavers	Sajjad Miah	LD	1990
Whitechapel	Abdul Asad	Lab	2002

2002 saw the boundary changes that lead to new opportunities arising, we now had 16 wards covered out of the 17. Please note, this table is not reflective of the election results for the period 2002-2010.

2014 -2018 Boundary (20 wards)

Wards	Councillors	Party	Date
Bethnal Green	Sirajul Islam	Lab	2014
Blackwall & Cubitt Town	Lutfur Rahman Ali	Lab	2002
Bromley South	Helal Uddin	Lab	2014
Bow East	Unsuccessful		
Bow West	Anwara Ali	Lab	2006
Bromley North	Khales Uddin Ahmed	Lab	2014
Canary Wharf	Md Maium Miah	Con	2014
Island Gardens	Unsuccessful		
Lansbury	Rajib Ahmed	Lab	2014
Limeouse	Soyful Alom	Lab	1994
Mile End	Shah Alam	PATH	2014
Poplar	Gulam Kibria Choudhury	IND	2014
Shadwell	Mrs Pola Uddin	Lab	1990
Spitalfields & Banglatown	Helal Uddn Abbas	Lab	2002
St Dunstan's	Jahangir Alam	Lab	1986
St Katharine's & Wapping	Shafiqul Haque	Lab	2002
St Peter's	Abdul Rahim	LD	1990
Stepney Green	Alibor Choudhury	Lab	2014
Weavers	Sajjad Miah	LD	1990
Whitechapel	Abdul Asad	Lab	2002

The boundary changes that took place in 2014 created 20 wards, three more than the previous boundry change in 2002. Few changes to the wards, such as amalgamations lead to further more opportunities.

St Katharine's ward merged with Wapping and so Md Ashik Ali remains assigned to St Katharine's, but this created another opportunity for another Bangladeshi to become another pioneer. This is the table as it stands for 2014 boundary change.

Bangladesh Connection

Zilah: Sylhet

Names	Balagoinj	Biswanath	Beani Bazar	Companygon	Fenchugonj	Kanaighat	Gulapgoinj	Kotwali/Tow	Gawainghat	Jaintiapur	Zakigoinj	Osmani
Abdul Asad			x									
Abdus Shukur							x					
Abjol Miah							x					
Ala Uddin								x				
Azizur Rahman		x										
Bodrul Md Alom							x					
Gulam K Choudhury												x
Khales Uddin Ahmed								x				
Lutfur Rahman												x
Md Sadik Ahmed												x
Mizanur Rahman												x
Mohammed Ali												x
Nuruddin Ahmed		x										
Ohid Ahmed							x					
Oliur Rahman												x
Rabina Khan												x
Raja Miah								x				
Rajib Ahmed							x					
Salim Ullah								x				
Shahab U Ahmed Belal			x									
Sherajul Haque							x					
Sirajul Islam		x										
Soyful Alom							x					
Sunawar Ali		x										
Waisel Islam							x					
Helal Uddin												x
Dulal Uddin		x										
Md Mamun Rashid			x									
Md Shahab Uddin			x									
Fanu Miah							x					
Total	0	5	5	0	0	0	9	4	0	0	0	8

Zillah: Sunamgoinj

Names	Sadar (Town)	Dowarabazar	Bishomborpur	Jagannathpur	Jamalgoinj	Sullah	Chhatak	Derai	Tahirpur
Abdal Ullah	x								
Abdul Matin				x					
Fazlul Haque				x					
Fozol Miah				x					
Gulam Mortuza				x					
Gulam Rabbani				x					
Helal Rahman				x					
Jusna Begum				x					
M. Maium Miah							x		
M A Mukit Chunu				x					
Mahbub Mamun Alam							x		
Md Abdullah Salique				x					
Mumtaz Samad				x					
Nasir Ahmed	x								
Shah Alam							x		
Suluk Ahmed				x					
Syed Nurul				x					
Zenith Rahman				x					
Abdul Aziz Sardar				x				x	
Alibor Choudhury				x					
Khaled Reza Khan								x	
Manir Uddin Ahmed				x					
Md Shahid Ali				x					
Sajjad Miah (Sajjadur)				x					
Total	2	0	0	19	0	0	3	2	0

Zillah: Hobigoinj

Names	Hobiganj Sadar	Nobiganj	Baniachong	Ajmiriganj	Lakhai	Madhabpur	Bahubal	Chunarughat
Md Mufti Miah		x						
Jahangir Alam (Jan)								x
Shafiqul Haque							x	
Syed A Mizan	x							
Alibor Choudhury		x						
Total	1	2	0	0	0	0	1	1

Zillah: Moulovi Bazar

Names	Maulvibazar	Barlekha	Raj Nagar	Kulaura	Kamalganj	Sree Mangal
Anamul Haque	x					
Ataur Rahman		x				
M A Rahim	x					
Md Jainal Uddin Choudhury		x				
Rajonuddin Jalal		x				
Sabina Akthar				x		
Shiria Khatun	x					
Total	3	3	0	1	0	0

Rest of the country

Name	Dhaka Dhanmond	Dhaka Tangail	Dhaka Jatra bari	Chittagong Feni	Rajshahi	Barisal	Comilla
Md Ashik Ali		x					
Md Nurul Huque				x			
Md Mustaquim			x				
Mrs P.M Uddin					x		
Ahmed Hussain							x
Lutfa Begum	x						
Rania Khan	x						
Kumar Murshid	x						

These tables are intended to paint a picture for the community and its people. While the politics is British, and for the British people, the British Bangladeshi community still has ancestral lineage to the 'homeland'.

It is also intended to formalise the progressiveness of the people in terms of where they originally arrived from. This knowledge is also intended for the future generations to look upon the pioneers and those that followed in admoration. How their people engaged in the political process coming from the 'homeland'.

APPENDIX

Elected Male Councillors:
Male List from 1982-2016

This table gives you the full list of elected male. We list them by date, their ward, their names and the party.

Year	Ward	First Name	Surname	Party
1982	St Katharine's	Mohammed Ashik	Ali	Lab
1982	Spitalfields	Mohammed Nurul	Huque	Ind
1985	Spitalfields	Abbas Helal	Uddin	Lab
1986	St Dunstan's	Jahangir (Jan)	Alam	Lab
1986	St Katharine's	Mohammed Ashik	Ali	Lab
1986	St Katharine's	Mohammed Sadik	Ahmed	Lab
1986	Spitalfields	Abbas Helal	Uddin	Lab
1986	Spitalfields	Mohammed Ghulam	Mortuza	Lab
1990	Holy Trinity	Akikur	Rahman	LD
1990	St Dunstan's	Shahab Uddin Belal	Ahmed	Lab
1990	St Katharine's	Abdul	Asad	Lab
1990	St Katharine's	Rajonuddin	Jalal	Lab
1990	St Katharine's	Shirajul	Islam	Lab
1990	St Peter's	Abdul	Rohim	LD
1990	Spitalfields	Mohammed Ghulam	Mortuza	Lab
1990	Spitalfields	Abbas Helal	Uddin	Lab
1990	Weavers	Sajjad	Miah	LD
1992	Spitalfields	Syed Aktaruzaman	Mizan	Lab
1994	Holy Trinity	Nuruddin	Ahmed	Lab
1994	Limehouse	Soyful	Alom	Lab
1994	St Dunstan's	Mohammed Shahab	Uddin	Lab
1994	St Katharine's	Abdul	Asad	Lab
1994	St Katharine's	Rajonuddin	Jalal	Lab
1994	Shadwell	Abdus	Shukur	Lab
1994	Spitalfields	Syed Aktaruzaman	Mizan	Lab
1994	Spitalfields	Mohammed Ghulam	Mortuza	Lab
1994	Spitalfields	Ataur	Rahman	Lab

1994	Weavers	Sunawar	Ali	Lab
1995	Spitalfields	Syed Aktaruzaman	Mizan	Lab
1995	Weavers	Mohammed	Ali	Lab
1998	Blackwall	Khan Ahmed Nuwayid (Kumar)	Murshid	Lab
1998	Bromley	Abdul Aziz	Sardar	Lab
1998	Limehouse	Helal Uddin	Abbas	Lab
1998	Limehouse	Soyful	Alom	Lab
1998	Redcoat	Ataur	Rahman	Lab
1998	St Katharine's	Abdul	Asad	Lab
1998	St Mary's	Motin	Uz-Zaman	Lab
1998	St Peter's	Raja	Miah	Lab
1998	Shadwell	Bodrul Mohammed	Alom	Lab
1998	Shadwell	Abdus	Shukur	Lab
1998	Spitalfields	Syed Aktaruzaman	Mizan	Lab
1998	Spitalfields	Mohammed Ghulam	Mortuza	Lab
1998	Spitalfields	Ala	Uddin	Lab
1998	Weavers	Mohammed	Ali	Lab
2001	Holy Trinity	Sirajul	Islam	Lab
2002	Bethnal Green North	Azizur Rahman	Khan	LD
2002	Bethnal Green South	Sirajul	Islam	Lab
2002	Bethnal Green South	Akikur	Rahman	LD
2002	Bethnal Green South	Salim	Ullah	Lab
2002	Blackwall & Cubitt Town	Lutfur Rahman	Ali	Lab
2002	Bromley-By-Bow	Abdul Aziz	Sardar	Lab
2002	Bromley-By-Bow	Khaled Reza	Khan	Lab
2002	East India & Lansbury	Ohid	Ahmed	Lab
2002	East India & Lansbury	Rajib	Ahmed	Lab

2002	Limehouse	Khan Ahmed Nuwayid (Kumar)	Murshid	Lab
2002	Mile End & Globe Town	Mohammed Jainal Uddin	Chowdhury	LD
2002	Mile End & Globe Town	Rofique Ullah	Ahmed	Lab
2002	Mile End East	Helal	Rahman	Lab
2002	Mile End East	Motin	Uz-Zaman	Lab
2002	Mile End East	Muhammad Abdullah	Salique	Lab
2002	Shadwell	Manir Uddin	Ahmed	Lab
2002	Shadwell	Abdus	Shukur	Lab
2002	Spitalfields & Banglatown	Helal Uddin	Abbas	Lab
2002	Spitalfields & Banglatown	Mohammed Ghulam	Mortuza	Lab
2002	Spitalfields & Banglatown	Lutfur	Rahman	Lab
2002	St Dunstan's & Stepney Green	Ataur	Rahman	Lab
2002	St Dunstan's & Stepney Green	Nasir	Uddin	Lab
2002	St Dunstan's & Stepney Green	Mohammed Shahab	Uddin	Lab
2002	St Katharine's & Wapping	Shafiqul	Haque	Lab
2002	Weavers	Mohammed Abdul	Matin	L D
2002	Whitechapel	Abdul	Asad	Lab
2002	Whitechapel	Fanu	Miah	Lab
2002	Whitechapel	Doros	Ullah	Lab
2006	Bethnal Green North	Muhammad Abdullah	Salique	Lab
2006	Bethnal Green North	Azizur Rahman	Khan	L D
2006	Bethnal Green South	Salim	Ullah	Lab
2006	Bethnal Green South	Sirajul	Islam	Lab
2006	Bromley-By-Bow	Abdul Aziz	Sardar	Lab

2006	Bromley-By-Bow	Mohammed Abdul	Munim	Res
2006	East Indian & Lansbury	Ohid	Ahmed	Lab
2006	East India & Lansbury	Rajib	Ahmed	LD
2006	Limehouse	Mohammed Shahid	Ali	Lab
2006	Limehouse	Dulal	Uddin	Res
2006	Mile End & Globe Town	Rofique Ullah	Ahmed	Lab
2006	Mile End East	Motin	Uz-Zaman	Lab
2006	Mile End East	Ahmed	Hussain	Res
2006	Shadwell	Shamim Ahmed	Choudhury	Res
2006	Shadwell	Abjol	Miah	Res
2006	Shadwell	Mohammed Mamun	Rashid	Res
2006	Spitalfields & Banglatown	Helal Uddin	Abbas	Lab
2006	Spitalfields & Banglatown	Fozol	Miah	Res
2006	Spitalfields & Banglatown	Lutfur	Rahman	Lab
2006	St Dunstan's & Stepney Green	Alibor	Choudhury	Lab
2006	St Dunstan's & Stepney Green	Abdal	Ullah	Lab
2006	St Dunstan's & Stepney Green	Oliur	Rahman	Res
2006	St Katharine's & Wapping	Shafiqul	Haque	Lab
2006	Weavers	Mohammed Abdul	Matin	LD
2006	Whitechapel	Shahed	Ali	Res
2006	Whitechapel	Abdul	Asad	Lab
2006	Whitechapel	Waiseul	Islam	Res
2008	Weavers	Fazlul	Haque	Lab
2010	Bethnal Green South	Mizanur Rahman	Choudhury	Lab
2010	Bethnal Green South	Sirajul	Islam	Lab

Year	Ward	First Name	Last Name	Party
2010	Bow West	Anwar Ahmed	Khan	Lab
2010	Bromley-By-Bow	Khales Uddin	Ahmed	Lab
2010	Bromley-By-Bow	Helal	Uddin	Lab
2010	East Indian & Lansbury	Ohid	Ahmed	Lab
2010	East Indian & Lansbury	Rajib	Ahmed	Lab
2010	Mile End & Globe Town	Rofique Ullah	Ahmed	Lab
2010	Mile End East	Motin	Uz-Zaman	Lab
2010	Mile End East	Kosru	Uddin	Lab
2010	Millwall	Md Maium	Miah	C
2010	Shadwell	Alibor	Choudhury	Lab
2010	Shadwell	Harun	Miah	Res
2010	Spitalfields & Banglatown	Lutfur	Rahman	Lab
2010	Spitalfields & Banglatown	Helal Uddin	Abbas	Lab
2010	St Dunstan's & Stepney Green	Abdal	Ullah	Lab
2010	St Dunstan's & Stepney Green	Oliur	Rahman	Lab
2010	St Katharine's & Wapping	Shafiqul	Haque	Lab
2010	Weavers	Kabir	Ahmed	Lab
2010	Weavers	Mohammed Abdul Mukit MBE		Lab
2010	Whitechapel	Shahed	Ali	Lab
2010	Whitechapel	Aminur	Khan	Lab
2010	Whitechapel	Abdul	Asad	Lab
2010	Spitalfields & Banglatown	Fozol	Miah	Res
2014	Bethnal Green	Sirajul	Islam	Lab
2014	Bethnal Green	Shafiqul	Haque	THF
2014	Bromley North	Khales Uddin	Ahmed	Lab
2014	Bromley North	Mohammed Mufti	Miah	THF

2014	Bromley South	Helal	Uddin	Lab
2014	Canary Wharf	Md Maium	Miah	THF
2014	Lansbury	Rajib	Ahmed	Lab
2014	Lansbury	Ohid	Ahmed	THF
2014	Mile End	Shah	Alam	THF
2014	St Peter's	Abjol	Miah	THF
2014	St Peter's	Muhammed Ansar	Mustaquim	THF
2014	Stepney Green	Alibor	Choudhury	THF
2014	Stepney Green	Oliur	Rahman	THF
2014	Weavers	Mohammed Abdul Chunu	Mukit MBE	Lab
2014	Whitechapel	Shahed	Ali	THF
2014	Whitechapel	Abdul	Asad	THF
2014	Whitechapel	Aminur	Khan	THF
2014	Shadwell	Harun	Miah	THF
2014	Spitalfields & Banglatown	Gulam	Rabbani	THF
2014	Spitalfields & Banglatown	Suluk	Ahmed	THF
2014	St Dunstan's	Ayas	Miah	Lab
2014	St Dunstan's	Mahbub Mamun	Alam	THF
2014	Poplar	Gulam Kibria	Chowdhury	THF
2016	Whitechapel	Shafi	Ahmed	Ind

Elected Female Councillors:

Female List from 1990-2016

Year	Ward	First Name	Surname	Party
1990	Shadwell	Mrs Pola Manzila	Uddin	Lab
1994	Shadwell	Mrs Pola Manzila	Uddin	Lab
1998	St Peter's	Jusna	Begum	Lab
2002	Millwall	Mumtaz	Samad	Lab
2006	Bow West	Anwara	Ali	Lab
2006	Bromley-By-Bow	Rania	Khan	Res
2006	East Indian & Lansbury	Shiria	Khatun	Lab
2006	Limehouse	Lutfa	Begum	Res
2010	Bethnal Green North	Zenith	Rahman	Lab
2010	Bromley-By-Bow	Rania	Khan	Lab
2010	East Indian & Lansbury	Shiria	Khatun	Lab
2010	Limehouse	Lutfa	Begum	Lab
2010	Shadwell	Rabina	Khan	Lab
2010	Spitalfields & Banglatown	Shelina	Akhtar	Lab
2014	Bow West	Asma	Begum	Lab
2014	Lansbury	Shiria	Khatun	Lab
2014	Shadwell	Rabina	Khan	THF
2015	Stepney Green	Sabina	Akthar	Lab

Full List:
All Bangladeshi Candidates

The table in this section list all the people who stood for election since 1982 male & female. There have been many ever since and are listed by the date, ward, their names and the party. In this table it does not indicated where they were elected or not.

Year	Ward	First Name	Surname	Party
1982	St Katherine's	Mohammed Ashik	Ali	Lab
1982	St Katherine's	Shahab Uddin Belal	Ahmed	Ind
1982	St Katherine's	Mohammed A.	Haque	Ind
1982	St Mary's	Rafique	Ullah	SDP
1982	St Mary's	Qudratul	Islam	SDP
1982	Spitalfields	Mohammed Nurul	Huque	Ind
1982	Spitalfields	Syed Nurul	Islam	Ind
1982	Spitalfields	Muhammed Ghulam	Mustafa	SDP
1982	Spitalfields	Abdul	Gofur	Ind
1982	Spitalfields	Sherajul	Hoque	Ind
1982	Weavers	Mohammed A.	Hussain	Ind
1985	Spitalfields	Helal Uddin	Abbas	Lab
1985	Spitalfields	M. Abdul	Hannan	Ind
1986	Blackwall	S	Ali	Lab
1986	Holy Trinity	Salim	Ullah	Lab
1986	St Dunstan's	Jahangir Jan	Alam	Lab
1986	St Katherine's	Mohammed Ashik	Ali	Lab
1986	St Katherine's	Mohammed Sadik	Ahmed	Lab
1986	St Katherine's	K	Ali	SDP
1986	St Katherine's	M	Hussain	SDP
1986	St Mary's	M	Ali	C
1986	Spitalfields	A	Uddin	Lab
1986	Spitalfields	Mohammed Ghulam	Mortuza	Lab
1986	Spitalfields	Mohammed Nurul	Huque	Ind
1986	Spitalfields	A	Rahman	SDP

1986	Spitalfields	S.F.	Islam	Ind
1986	Spitalfields	Mohammed Ghulam	Mustafa	SDP
1986	Weavers	M.B.H.	Ludi	Lab
1988	St Katherine's	Anhar	Uddin	SDP
1990	Holy Trinity	Akikur	Rahman	LD
1990	Holy Trinity	Sunawar	Ali	Lab
1990	Limehouse	Khan Ahmed Nuwayid (Kumar)	Murshid	Lab
1990	Redcoat	A	Ali	Lab
1990	Redcoat	A.M	Khan	Ind
1990	St Dunstan's	Shahab Uddin Belal	Ahmed	Lab
1990	St Katherine's	Abdul	Asad	Lab
1990	St Katherine's	Rajonuddin	Jalal	Lab
1990	St Katherine's	Shirajul	Islam	Lab
1990	St Katherine's	Abdul	Hamid	C
1990	St Katherine's	A.U.	Ahmed	CC
1990	St Katherine's	M	Anas	CC
1990	St Mary's	S.M.	Hoque	CC
1990	St Mary's	Abu Hamid Mohammed Equbal	Hossain	Ind
1990	St Mary's	M.A.S.	Khan	C
1990	St Peter's	Sajjadur	Miah	L D
1990	St Peter's	F.	Miah	Lab
1990	Shadwell	Mrs Paula Manzila	Uddin	Lab
1990	Spitalfields	Mohammed Ghulam	Mortuza	Lab
1990	Spitalfields	Ala	Uddin	Lab
1990	Spitalfields	A	Kadir	C
1990	Spitalfields	A.M	Khan	CC
1990	Weavers	Sajjadur	Miah	L D
1990	Weavers	S.	Islam	Lab
1990	Weavers	Mohammed Abdul	Rakib	Ind
1990	Weavers	S.M.	Ali	C
1990	Weavers	S	Uddin	C
1992	Spitalfields	Syed Aktaruzaman	Mizan	Lab

1994	Holy Trinity	Nuruddin	Ahmed	Lab
1994	Holy Trinity	A	Rahman	L D
1994	Limehouse	Soyful	Alom	Lab
1994	Limehouse	M.T	Khan	Ind
1994	Limehouse	S	Samih	C
1994	St Dunstan's	Mohammed Shahab	Uddin	Lab
1994	St Dunstan's	A.M	Khan	L D
1994	St Dunstan's	M	Miah	Ind
1994	St Katherine's	Abdul	Asad	Lab
1994	St Katherine's	Rajonuddin	Jalal	Lab
1994	St Katherine's	A.H.S.	Miah	L D
1994	St Katherine's	A.H.	Ali	Ind Lab
1994	St Mary's	Bodrul Mohammed	Alom	Lab
1994	St Mary's	A	Ali	L D
1994	St Mary's	Mohammed A.S.	Khan	C
1994	St Peter's	Ala	Uddin	Lab
1994	St Peter's	S.S.	Islam	L D
1994	Shadwell	Mrs Pola Manzila	Uddin	Lab
1994	Shadwell	Abdus	Shukur	Lab
1994	Shadwell	H.	Miah	L D
1994	Shadwell	A	Miah	Ind Lab
1994	Spitalfields	Syed Akhtaruzzaman	Mizan	Lab
1994	Spitalfields	Mohammed Ghulam	Mortuza	Lab
1994	Spitalfields	Ataur	Rahman	Lab
1994	Spitalfields	Mohammed Nurul	Huque	L D
1994	Spitalfields	Syed Nurul	Islam	L D
1994	Spitalfields	Mohammed Abdul	Matin	L D
1994	Spitalfields	Ullah	Mohi	Ind Lab
1994	Weavers	Sunawar	Ali	Lab
1994	Weavers	N	Uddin	Ind LD
1994	Weavers	S	Miah	L D
1995	Spitalfields	Syed Akhtaruzzaman	Mizan	Lab
1995	Weavers	Mohammed	Ali	Lab

1995	Weavers	S	Miah	L D
1996	St Mary's	Reza Shafi	Choudhury	C
1998	Blackwall	Khan Ahmed Nuwayid (Kumar)	Murshid	Lab
1998	Bromley	Abdul Aziz	Sardar	Lab
1998	East India	Rajib	Ahmed	Lab
1998	Grove	Syed Enamul	Hoque	C
1998	Holy Trinity	Salim	Ullah	Lab
1998	Holy Trinity	M.A.	Syed	C
1998	Limehouse	Helal Uddin	Abbas	Lab
1998	Limehouse	Soyful	Alom	Lab
1998	Limehouse	Abu Hamid Mohammed Equbal	Hossain	Ind
1998	Limehouse	Parvin	Begum	Ind
1998	Limehouse	Motiur	Rahman	C
1998	Redcoat	Ataur	Rahman	Lab
1998	St Dunstan's	Shahab Uddin Belal	Ahmed	Lab
1998	St Dunstan's	Mohammed Shahab	Uddin	Lab
1998	St James	Mohammed Hashmot	Ullah	C
1998	St Katherine's	Abdul	Asad	Lab
1998	St Katherine's	Anamul	Hoque	Lab
1998	St Katherine's	Mostofa	Miah	C
1998	St Katherine's	Hilal	Miah	L D
1998	St Mary's	Motin	Uz-Zaman	Lab
1998	St Mary's	Habibur Rahman	Choudhury	C
1998	St Peter's	Jusna	Begum	Lab
1998	St Peter's	Raja	Miah	Lab
1998	St Peter's	Mohammed Jainal Uddin	Choudhury	L D
1998	Shadwell	Bodrul Mohammed	Alom	Lab
1998	Shadwell	Abdus	Shukur	Lab
1998	Shadwell	Abdul	Malik	Ind
1998	Spitalfields	Syed Akhtaruzzaman	Mizan	Lab
1998	Spitalfields	Mohammed Ghulam	Mortuzza	Lab
1998	Spitalfields	Ala	Uddin	Lab

1998	Spitalfields	E	Shaikh	C
1998	Weavers	Mohammed	Ali	Lab
1998	Weavers	Abdul Majid	Khan	L D
1998	Weavers	Mohammed Shahab	Uddin	C
2001	Holy Trinity	Sirajul	Islam	Lab
2002	Bethnal Green North	Azizur Rahman	Khan	L D
2002	Bethnal Green North	Raja	Miah	Lab
2002	Bethnal Green North	Sajjadur	Rahman	C
2002	Bethnal Green South	Sirajul	Islam	Lab
2002	Bethnal Green South	Akikur	Rahman	L D
2002	Bethnal Green South	Salim	Ullah	Lab
2002	Bethnal Green South	Nurul	Karim	L D
2002	Bethnal Green South	Shahin	Ahmed	C
2002	Bethnal Green South	Anamul	Haque	C
2002	Blackwall & Cubitt Town	Lutfur Rahman	Ali	Lab
2002	Bow East	Ala	Uddin	Lab
2002	Bow East	Kazi Nazmul	Alam	C
2002	BromleyByBow	Abdul Aziz	Sardar	Lab
2002	BromleyByBow	Khaled Reza	Khan	Lab
2002	BromleyByBow	Abdul	Mannan	L Dem
2002	East India & Lansbury	Ohid	Ahmed	Lab
2002	East India & Lansbury	Rajib	Ahmed	Lab
2002	East India & Lansbury	Mohammed Azizul	Haque	Ind
2002	Limehouse	Khan Ahmed Nuwayid (Kumar)	Murshid	Lab
2002	Mile End & Globe Town	Mohammed Jainal Uddin	Chowdhury	LD
2002	Mile End & Globe Town	Rofique U	Ahmed	Lab

2002	Mile End & Globe Town	Sharmin	Shajahan	Lab
2002	Mile End & Globe Town	Jahidul	Hoque	C
2002	Mile End & Globe Town	Mohammed Rezaul	Karim	C
2002	Mile End East	Helal	Rahman	Lab
2002	Mile End East	Motin	Uz-Zaman	Lab
2002	Mile End East	Muhammad Abdullah	Salique	Lab
2002	Mile End East	Mohammed Sazzadur	Rahman	LD
2002	Millwall	Mumtaz	Samad	Lab
2002	Shadwell	Manir Uddin	Ahmed	Lab
2002	Shadwell	Abdus	Shukur	Lab
2002	Shadwell	Nanu	Miah	LD
2002	Spitalfields & Banglatown	Helal Uddin	Abbas	Lab
2002	Spitalfields & Banglatown	Mohammed Ghulam	Mortuzza	Lab
2002	Spitalfields & Banglatown	Lutfur	Rahman	Lab
2002	Spitalfields & Banglatown	Md Azizur Dara	Rahman	C
2002	Spitalfields & Banglatown	Pir Md Abdul	Quium	C
2002	Spitalfields & Banglatown	Ahmed	Hussain	C
2002	Spitalfields & Banglatown	Alas	Uddin	LD
2002	Spitalfields & Banglatown	Muhit	Ahmed	Ind
2002	Spitalfields & Banglatown	Ismail Khubaib	Malik	Ind
2002	Spitalfields & Banglatown	Sultan	Ahmed	Ind
2002	St Dunstan's & Stepney Green	Ataur	Rahman	Lab
2002	St Dunstan's & Stepney Green	Nasir	Uddin	Lab
2002	St Dunstan's & Stepney Green	Mohammed Shahab	Uddin	Lab
2002	St Dunstan's & Stepney Green	Hafizur	Rahman	C

Year	Ward	First Name	Surname	Party
2002	St Dunstan's & Stepney Green	Shamim Ahmed	Choudhury	C
2002	St Dunstan's & Stepney Green	Muhammade Mominul	Hoque	C
2002	St Dunstan's & Stepney Green	Mohibur	Rahman	L D
2002	St Katherine's & Wapping	Shafiqul	Haque	Lab
2002	St Katherine's & Wapping	Mohammed Farid Uddin	Ahmed	L D
2002	Weavers	Mohammed Abdul	Matin	L D
2002	Weavers	Sirajul	Islam	Lab
2002	Weavers	Humaiun	Kobir	Lab
2002	Weavers	Mohammed Abdul	Kadir	C
2002	Whitechapel	Abdul	Asad	Lab
2002	Whitechapel	Fanu	Miah	Lab
2002	Whitechapel	Doros	Ullah	Lab
2002	Whitechapel	Mostofa	Miah	C
2002	Whitechapel	Shafique	Miah	C
2002	Whitechapel	Monsur Azad	Ahmed	C
2002	Whitechapel	Mohammed Zaki	Ahmed	Ind
2002	Whitechapel	Shamsuddin	Ahmed	Ind
2002	Whitechapel	Anu	Miah	Ind
2002	Whitechapel	Sajaul	Karim	L D
2002	Whitechapel	Gulam	Hussain	L D
2006	Bethnal Green North	Muhammad Abdullah	Salique	Lab
2006	Bethnal Green North	Azizur Rahman	Khan	L D
2006	Bethnal Green North	Abu Sufian	Choudhury	Res
2006	Bethnal Green North	Syed Ashraf	Hussain	Res
2006	Bethnal Green North	Jamal Ahmed	Khan	C
2006	Bethnal Green North	Shamsu	Miah	C
2006	Bethnal Green North	Nishat	Kabir	C
2006	Bethnal Green	Salim	Ullah	Lab

		South		
2006	Bethnal Green South	Sirajul	Islam	Lab
2006	Bethnal Green South	Syeda Nurun Nahar	Hussain	Res
2006	Bethnal Green South	Afzal	Mahmood	Res
2006	Bethnal Green South	Akikur	Rahman	LD
2006	Bethnal Green South	Mohammed Fazlul	Rahman	L D
2006	Bethnal Green South	Mohammed Nanu	Miah	LD
2006	Bethnal Green South	Moynul Haque	Choudhury	C
2006	Blackwall & Cubitt Town	Shofu	Miah	LD
2006	Blackwall & Cubitt Town	Abdul Kahar	Choudhury	Res
2006	Blackwall & Cubitt Town	Aysha	Ali	Res
2006	Blackwall & Cubitt Town	Jahidul	Hoque	LD
2006	Blackwall & Cubitt Town	Shamsur Rahman	Choudhury	Ind
2006	Blackwall & Cubitt Town	Shelima	Choudhury	Ind
2006	Blackwall & Cubitt Town	Najma	Rahman	Ind
2006	Bow West	Anwara	Ali	Lab
2006	Bow West	Anwar	Hussain	C
2006	Bromley-By-Bow	Abdul Aziz	Sardar	Lab
2006	Bromley-By-Bow	Rania	Khan	Res
2006	Bromley-By-Bow	Mohammed Abdul	Munim	Res
2006	Bromley-By-Bow	Helal	Rahman	Ind
2006	Bromley-By-Bow	Khaled Reza	Khan	Ind
2006	Bromley-By-Bow	Koyes Uzzaman	Choudhury	LD
2006	Bromley-By-Bow	Mohammod Jalal	Uddin	LD
2006	Bromley-By-Bow	Kazi Nazmul	Alam	C
2006	East Indian & Lansbury	Shiria	Khatun	Lab

2006	East Indian & Lansbury	Ohid	Ahmed	Lab
2006	East India & Lansbury	Rajib	Ahmed	LD
2006	East Indian & Lansbury	Iqbal	Hossain	LD
2006	East Indian & Lansbury	Mohammed Abdus	Shahid	Res
2006	East Indian & Lansbury	Mahfuz Ahmed	Khan	Ind
2006	Limehouse	Mohammed Shahid	Ali	Lab
2006	Limehouse	Lutfa	Begum	Res
2006	Limehouse	Dulal	Uddin	Res
2006	Limehouse	Mohammed Aminul	Haque	Ind
2006	Limehouse	Abdul	Jamal	Ind
2006	Limehouse	Husheara	Begum	LD
2006	Mile End & Globe Town	Rofique U	Ahmed	Lab
2006	Mile End & Globe Town	Mehdi	Hassan	Res
2006	Mile End & Globe Town	Mohammed Jainal Uddin	Chowdhury	LD
2006	Mile End & Globe Town	Partab	Ali	L D
2006	Mile End & Globe Town	Kobir	Ahmed	C
2006	Mile End East	Motin	Uz-Zaman	Lab
2006	Mile End East	Ahmed	Hussain	Res
2006	Mile End East	Misbahur Rahman	Khan	L D
2006	Mile End East	Ismail	Hussain	Res
2006	Mile End East	Shamsul Islam	Syed	L D
2006	Mile End East	Hafizur Rahman	Choudhury	Ind
2006	Mile End East	Jewel	Islam	C
2006	Millwall	Arip	Miah	Lab
2006	Millwall	Mohammed Shah Saiful	Alam-Raja	Res
2006	Shadwell	Shamim Ahmed	Choudhury	Res
2006	Shadwell	Abjol	Miah	Res
2006	Shadwell	Mohammed Mamun	Rashid	Res

2006	Shadwell	Humayun	Kabir	Lab
2006	Shadwell	Abdus	Shukur	Lab
2006	Shadwell	Sajjadur	Rahman	C
2006	Shadwell	Mohammed	Ali	L D
2006	Spitalfields & Banglatown	Helal Uddin	Abbas	Lab
2006	Spitalfields & Banglatown	Fozol	Miah	Res
2006	Spitalfields & Banglatown	Lutfur	Rahman	Lab
2006	Spitalfields & Banglatown	Mohammed Ghulam	Mortuzza	Lab
2006	Spitalfields & Banglatown	Mizanur Rahman	Choudhury	Ind
2006	Spitalfields & Banglatown	Mohammed Badrul	Islam	Res
2006	Spitalfields & Banglatown	Mohammed Yousuf	Kamali	L D
2006	Spitalfields & Banglatown	Mohammed Abdul Mukith	Choudhury	Res
2006	Spitalfields & Banglatown	Dinul Hussain	Shah	C
2006	Spitalfields & Banglatown	Mohammed Aminur	Rahman	L D
2006	Spitalfields & Banglatown	Iqbal	Hussain	C
2006	Spitalfields & Banglatown	Hamid Ur-Rahman	Chowdhury	C
2006	St Dunstan's & Stepney Green	Alibor	Choudhury	Lab
2006	St Dunstan's & Stepney Green	Abdal	Ullah	Lab
2006	St Dunstan's & Stepney Green	Oliur	Rahman	Res
2006	St Dunstan's & Stepney Green	Mohammed Shahab	Uddin	Lab
2006	St Dunstan's & Stepney Green	Aleyk	Miah	Res
2006	St Dunstan's & Stepney Green	Habibur	Rahman	L D
2006	St Dunstan's & Stepney Green	Ataur	Rahman	Ind
2006	St Dunstan's & Stepney Green	Ahmed	Mustaque	L D

2006	St Dunstan's & Stepney Green	Farid Uddin	Ahmed	L D
2006	St Katherine's & Wapping	Shafiqul	Haque	Lab
2006	Weavers	Mohammed Abdul	Matin	L D
2006	Weavers	Fazlul	Haque	Lab
2006	Weavers	Dilwara	Begum	Res
2006	Weavers	Gias Uddin	Ahmed	Ind
2006	Weavers	Hamida Rahman	Chowdhury	C
2006	Whitechapel	Shahed	Ali	Res
2006	Whitechapel	Abdul	Asad	Lab
2006	Whitechapel	Waiseul	Islam	Res
2006	Whitechapel	Lutfur	Rahman	Lab
2006	Whitechapel	Doros	Ullah	Lab
2006	Whitechapel	Farhana	Zaman	Res
2006	Whitechapel	Fanu	Miah	Ind
2006	Whitechapel	Mohammed Sultan	Haydar	L D
2006	Whitechapel	Shamsuddin	Ahmed	L D
2006	Whitechapel	Muhammed Shafique	Ahmed	C
2006	Whitechapel	Shah Mohammed Shuhel	Rezaul	C
2006	Whitechapel	Mohammed Abdul	Goni	Ind
2008	Millwall	Doros	Ullah	Lab
2008	Millwall	Mohammed Nasir	Uddin	L D
2008	Millwall	Reza	Mehbob	Res
2008	Weavers	Fazlul	Haque	Lab
2008	Weavers	Dilwara	Begum	Res
2008	Weavers	Gias Uddin	Ahmed	C
2008	Weavers	Niru Murshid	Murshid	Ind
2008	Mile End East	Motiur	Rahman	C
2008	Mile End East	Hafiz	Choudhury	Res
2008	Mile End East	Jainal	Choudhury	L D
2010	Bethnal Green North	Zenith	Rahman	Lab
2010	Bethnal Green North	Muhammad Abdullah	Salique	Lab

2010	Bethnal Green North	Azizur Rahman	Khan	L D
2010	Bethnal Green North	Muhammad Ansar Pramanik	Ali	Res
2010	Bethnal Green North	Nur	Baksh	C
2010	Bethnal Green North	Syedun	Noor	Res
2010	Bethnal Green North	Shirin Samanta	Akhter	Res
2010	Bethnal Green South	Mizanur Rahman	Choudhury	Lab
2010	Bethnal Green South	Sirajul	Islam	Lab
2010	Bethnal Green South	Salim	Ullah	Res
2010	Bethnal Green South	Abu Hamza Afzal	Mahmood	Res
2010	Bethnal Green South	Monjur	Ali	Res
2010	Bethnal Green South	Rahena	Anisha	L D
2010	Bethnal Green South	Mohammed Nasir	Uddin	L D
2010	Bethnal Green South	Salina	Begum	C
2010	Bethnal Green South	Noor	Miah	C
2010	Blackwall & Cubitt Town	Waiseul	Islam	Lab
2010	Blackwall & Cubitt Town	Gulam Kibria	Choudhury	Res
2010	Blackwall & Cubitt Town	Mohammed	Rahman	Res
2010	Blackwall & Cubitt Town	Abdul	Malik	Res
2010	Bow East	Rafique	ullah	L D
2010	Bow East	Mujibur	Rahman	Res
2010	Bow East	Emdadul Imran	Haque	Ind
2010	Bow West	Anwar Ahmed	Khan	Lab
2010	Bow West	Anwara	Ali	C
2010	Bow West	Jainal	Choudhury	L D
2010	Bow West	Syed	Islam	Res

2010	Bromley-By-Bow	Khales Uddin	Ahmed	Lab
2010	Bromley-By-Bow	Rania	Khan	Lab
2010	Bromley-By-Bow	Helal	Uddin	Lab
2010	Bromley-By-Bow	Subrina	Hossain	C
2010	Bromley-By-Bow	Bodrul	Islam	Res
2010	Bromley-By-Bow	Shamima	Begum	L D
2010	Bromley-By-Bow	Alkas	Hoque	L D
2010	Bromley-By-Bow	Mohammed Mufti	Miah	Res
2010	Bromley-By-Bow	Kamal	Uddin	Res
2010	Bromley-By-Bow	Koyes Uzzaman	Choudhury	L D
2010	East Indian & Lansbury	Ohid	Ahmed	Lab
2010	East Indian & Lansbury	Shiria	Khatun	Lab
2010	East Indian & Lansbury	Rajib	Ahmed	Lab
2010	East Indian & Lansbury	Iqbal	Hossain	L D
2010	East Indian & Lansbury	Kamrul	Hussain	Res
2010	East Indian & Lansbury	Zakir	Hussain	Res
2010	East Indian & Lansbury	Ahmed	Mustaque	C
2010	East Indian & Lansbury	Zillur	Uddin	L D
2010	East Indian & Lansbury	Zak	Ali	L D
2010	Limehouse	Lutfa	Begum	Lab
2010	Limehouse	Dulal	Uddin	Res
2010	Limehouse	Hafiza	Islam	Res
2010	Limehouse	Sakib	Ershad	C
2010	Limehouse	Anfor	Ali	Res
2010	Limehouse	Hafizur Mohammed	Rahman	L D
2010	Limehouse	Faruk	Chowdhury	L D
2010	Limehouse	Muazzam	Rakol	L D
2010	Mile End & Globe Town	Rofique U	Ahmed	Lab

2010	Mile End & Globe Town	Shamsul	Haque	L D
2010	Mile End & Globe Town	Rafique	Ahmed	L D
2010	Mile End & Globe Town	Syed Shikul	Islam	L D
2010	Mile End & Globe Town	Ahad Ahmed	Chowdhury	Res
2010	Mile End & Globe Town	Muhammed Khoyrul	Shaheed	C
2010	Mile End & Globe Town	Habib	Rahman	Res
2010	Mile End East	Motin	Uz-Zaman	Lab
2010	Mile End East	Kosru	Uddin	Lab
2010	Mile End East	Ahmed	Hussain	C
2010	Mile End East	Mohammed Altaf	Rahmani	Res
2010	Mile End East	Hafiz	Choudhury	L D
2010	Mile End East	Jamir	Choudhury	Res
2010	Mile End East	Bodrul Islam	Choudhury	C
2010	Mile End East	Altaf	Hussain	L D
2010	Mile End East	Fiyaz	Ali	Res
2010	Mile End East	Kamrun	Shajahan	L D
2010	Millwall	Md Maium	Miah	C
2010	Millwall	Doros	Ullah	Lab
2010	Millwall	Shuily	Begum	Res
2010	Millwall	Muzibul	Islam	Res
2010	Shadwell	Alibor	Choudhury	Lab
2010	Shadwell	Harun	Miah	Res
2010	Shadwell	Rabina	Khan	Lab
2010	Shadwell	Khaled Reza	Khan	C
2010	Shadwell	Mohammed Mamun	Rashid	Res
2010	Shadwell	Nasima	Begum	C
2010	Shadwell	Monjur	Alam	Res
2010	Shadwell	Muhammed Nazrul	Alom	L D
2010	Shadwell	Jewel	Choudhury	L D
2010	Shadwell	Mostaque	Hussain	LD

2010	Spitalfields & Banglatown	Lutfur	Rahman	Lab
2010	Spitalfields & Banglatown	Shelina	Akhtar	Lab
2010	Spitalfields & Banglatown	Helal Uddin	Abbas	Lab
2010	Spitalfields & Banglatown	Fozol	Miah	Res
2010	Spitalfields & Banglatown	Moniruzzaman	Syed	L D
2010	Spitalfields & Banglatown	Sadek	Khan	C
2010	Spitalfields & Banglatown	Jewel Toropdar	Ahmed	L D
2010	Spitalfields & Banglatown	Asad	Ahmod	C
2010	Spitalfields & Banglatown	Ahad	Ali	Res
2010	Spitalfields & Banglatown	Mohammed Salim	Hossain	G
2010	Spitalfields & Banglatown	Shah	Yousuf	Ind
2010	St Dunstan's & Stepney Green	Abdal	Ullah	Lab
2010	St Dunstan's & Stepney Green	Oliur	Rahman	Lab
2010	St Dunstan's & Stepney Green	Mahbub Mamun	Alam	Res
2010	St Dunstan's & Stepney Green	Abul	Hussain	Res
2010	St Dunstan's & Stepney Green	Shahar	Imran	Res
2010	St Dunstan's & Stepney Green	Aleyk	Miah	C
2010	St Dunstan's & Stepney Green	Ahbab	Miah	L D
2010	St Dunstan's & Stepney Green	Sufian	Choudhury	L D
2010	St Dunstan's & Stepney Green	Harun	Rashid	C
2010	St Dunstan's & Stepney Green	Mohammed Shahab	Uddin	Ind
2010	St Katherine's & Wapping	Shafiqul	Haque	Lab
2010	St Katherine's & Wapping	Muhammad Abdul Hye	Choudhury	Res

2010	St Katherine's & Wapping	Quadri	Mamun	L D
2010	St Katherine's & Wapping	Muhammed Shafiq	Islam	Res
2010	St Katherine's & Wapping	Dilwara	Ali	Res
2010	Weavers	Kabir	Ahmed	Lab
2010	Weavers	Mohammed Abdul MBE	Mukit	Lab
2010	Weavers	Sajjadur	Miah	L D
2010	Weavers	Yousuf	Khan	Res
2010	Weavers	Fazlul	Haque	Res
2010	Weavers	Akhtar Imran	Ahmed	C
2010	Weavers	Gias Uddin	Ahmed	C
2010	Whitechapel	Shahed	Ali	Lab
2010	Whitechapel	Aminur	Khan	Lab
2010	Whitechapel	Abdul	Asad	Lab
2010	Whitechapel	Saleh	Ahmed	L D
2010	Whitechapel	Lutfur	Rahman	Res
2010	Whitechapel	Kamal Uddin	Ali	L D
2010	Whitechapel	Ahad	Abdul	C
2010	Whitechapel	Fanu	Miah	C
2010	Whitechapel	Shamim	Rahman	L D
2010	Whitechapel	Saidul	Alom	Res
2010	Whitechapel	Mohammed Shahab	Uddin	G
2010	Spitalfields & Banglatown	Fozol	Miah	Res
2012	Spitalfields & Banglatown	Abdul	Alim	Lab
2012	Spitalfields & Banglatown	Jewel	Choudhury	Ind
2014	Bethnal Green	Sirajul	Islam	Lab
2014	Bethnal Green	Shafiqul	Haque	THF
2014	Bethnal Green	Babu	Choudhury	THF
2014	Bethnal Green	Salim	Ullah	THF
2014	Bethnal Green	Kamrun	Shajahan	L D
2014	Bethnal Green	Taz	Khalique	C

2014	Blackwall & Cubitt Town	Anusur	Rahman	Lab
2014	Blackwall & Cubitt Town	Faruk	Khan	THF
2014	Blackwall & Cubitt Town	Kabir	Ahmed	THF
2014	Blackwall & Cubitt Town	Mohammed	Aktaruzzaman	THF
2014	Blackwall & Cubitt Town	Mohammed Akhlaqur	Rahman	Ind
2014	Bow East	Sabia	Kamali	THF
2014	Bow East	Abdus	Salam	THF
2014	Bow West	Asma	Begum	Lab
2014	Bow West	Jainal	Chowdhury	THF
2014	Bow West	Anwar Ahmed	Khan	Ind
2014	Bow West	S. M Saiful	Azam	C
2014	Bow West	Altaf	Hussain	L D
2014	Bromley North	Khales Uddin	Ahmed	Lab
2014	Bromley North	Mohammed Mufti	Miah	THF
2014	Bromley North	Zenith	Rahman	Lab
2014	Bromley North	Moniruzzaman	Syed	THF
2014	Bromley South	Helal	Uddin	Lab
2014	Bromley South	Syeda	Choudhury	THF
2014	Bromley South	Kabir	Ali	THF
2014	Canary Wharf	Md Maium	Miah	THF
2014	Canary Wharf	Shubo	Hussain	Lab
2014	Canary Wharf	Ahmed	Hussain	C
2014	Island Garden	Raju	Rahman	Lab
2014	Island Garden	Belal	Rahman	THF
2014	Limehouse	Mashuk	Ahmed	THF
2014	Lansbury	Rajib	Ahmed	Lab
2014	Lansbury	Shiria	Khatun	Lab
2014	Lansbury	Ohid	Ahmed	THF
2014	Lansbury	Shuily	Akthar	THF
2014	Lansbury	Mohammed	Riaz	C
2014	Mile End	Shah	Alam	THF

2014	Mile End	Mohammed Shaid	Ali	THF
2014	Mile End	Motin	Uz-Zaman	Lab
2014	Mile End	Mustak	Syed	THF
2014	Mile End	Mushtak	Abdullah	C
2014	Mile End	Jewel	Islam	C
2014	Mile End	Hafiz	Choudhury	Ind
2014	Mile End	Arzoo	Miah	TUSC
2014	St Katherine's & Wapping	Ahad	Miah	THF
2014	St Peter's	Abjol	Miah	THF
2014	St Peter's	Muhammed Ansar	Mustaquim	THF
2014	St Peter's	Aktaruz	Zaman	THF
2014	St Peter's	Sanu	Miah	Lab
2014	St Peter's	Azizur Rahman	Khan	L D
2014	Stepney Green	Alibor	Choudhury	THF
2014	Stepney Green	Oliur	Rahman	THF
2014	Stepney Green	Sabina	Akthar	Lab
2014	Weavers	Mohammed Abdul MBE	Mukit	Lab
2014	Weavers	Kabir	Ahmed	THF
2014	Weavers	Yousuf	Khan	THF
2014	Whitechapel	Shahed	Ali	THF
2014	Whitechapel	Abdul	Asad	THF
2014	Whitechapel	Aminur	Khan	THF
2014	Whitechapel	Faruque Mahfuz	Ahmed	Lab
2014	Whitechapel	Jamalur	Rahman	Lab
2014	Shadwell	Rabina	Khan	THF
2014	Shadwell	Harun	Miah	THF
2014	Shadwell	Mohammed Mamun	Rashid	Lab
2014	Shadwell	Farhana	Zaman	Lab
2014	Shadwell	Monowara	Begum	L D
2014	Spitalfields & Banglatown	Gulam	Rabbani	THF
2014	Spitalfields & Banglatown	Suluk	Ahmed	THF
2014	Spitalfields &	Helal Uddin	Abbas	Lab

	Banglatown			
2014	Spitalfields & Banglatown	Tarik	Khan	Lab
2014	St Dunstan's	Ayas	Miah	Lab
2014	St Dunstan's	Mahbub Mamun	Alam	THF
2014	St Dunstan's	Abdal	Ullah	Lab
2014	St Dunstan's	Rofique U	Ahmed	THF
2014	St Dunstan's	Abdul Munim	Choudhury	T P P
2014	St Dunstan's	Koyes Uzzaman	Choudhury	L D
2014	Poplar	Gulam Kibria	Chowdhury	THF
2014	Poplar	Abdul Kahar	Chowdhury	Lab
2015	Stepney Green	Sabina	Akthar	Lab
2015	Stepney Green	Abu Talha Chowdhury	Choudhury	Ind
2015	Stepney Green	Saiful	Azam	C
2016	Whitechapel	Shafi	Ahmed	Ind

List of all Bangladeshi Female Candidates

This table list all female candidates since 1990, but does not indicate whether elected or not. This separate list is to give them their own space, and to recognise their achievements and their determination to be in the public domain, equal to the men.

Year	Ward	First Name	Surname	Party
1990	Shadwell	Mrs Paula Manzila	Uddin	Lab
1994	Shadwell	Mrs Paula Manzila	Uddin	Lab
1998	Limehouse	Parvin	Begum	Ind
1998	St Peter's	Jusna	Begum	Lab
2002	Millwall	Mumtaz	Samad	Lab
2006	Bethnal Green North	Nishat	Kabir	C
2006	Bethnal Green South	Syeda Nurun Nahar	Hussain	Res
2006	Blackwall & Cubitt Town	Aysha	Ali	Res
2006	Blackwall & Cubitt Town	Shelima	Choudhury	Ind
2006	Blackwall & Cubitt Town	Najma	Rahman	Ind
2006	Bow West	Anwara	Ali	Lab
2006	Bromley-By-Bow	Rania	Khan	Res
2006	East Indian & Lansbury	Shiria	Khatun	Lab
2006	Limehouse	Lutfa	Begum	Res
2006	Limehouse	Husheara	Begum	LD
2006	Weavers	Dilwara	Begum	Res
2006	Weavers	Hamida Rahman	Chowdhury	C
2008	Weavers	Dilwara	Begum	Res
2008	Weavers	Niru Murshid	Murshid	Ind
2010	Bethnal Green North	Syedun	Noor	Res
2010	Bethnal Green North	Shirin Samanta	Akhter	Res
2010	Bethnal Green South	Rahena	Anisha	LD
2010	Bethnal Green South	Salina	Begum	C

Year	Ward	First Name	Surname	Party
2010	Bow West	Anwara	Ali	C
2010	Bromley-By-Bow	Rania	Khan	Lab
2010	Bromley-By-Bow	Subrina	Hossain	C
2010	Bromley-By-Bow	Shamima	Begum	LD
2010	East Indian & Lansbury	Shiria	Khatun	Lab
2010	Limehouse	Lutfa	Begum	Lab
2010	Limehouse	Hafiza	Islam	Res
2010	Mile End East	Kamrun	Shajahan	LD
2010	Millwall	Shuily	Begum	Res
2010	Shadwell	Rabina	Khan	Lab
2010	Shadwell	Nasima	Begum	C
2010	Spitalfields & Banglatown	Shelina	Akhtar	Lab
2010	St Katherine's & Wapping	Dilwara	Ali	Res
2014	Bow East	Sabia	Kamali	THF
2014	Bow West	Asma	Begum	Lab
2014	Bromley North	Zenith	Rahman	Lab
2014	Bromley South	Syeda	Choudhury	THF
2014	Lansbury	Shiria	Khatun	Lab
2014	Lansbury	Shuily	Akthar	THF
2014	Stepney Green	Sabina	Akthar	Lab
2014	Shadwell	Rabina	Khan	THF
2014	Shadwell	Farhana	Zaman	Lab
2014	Shadwell	Monowara	Begum	LD
2015	Stepney Green	Sabina	Akthar	Lab

Political Pathfinders

Tower Hamlet's Election Results
by Ward MAP 1982-2016

Community Progression

Here we have a set of maps of the borough to give an overview of how the boroughs voting composition shaped up.

1982-1986 Election

1986-1990 Election

1990-1994 Election

1994-1998 Election

1998-2002 Election

2002-2006 Election

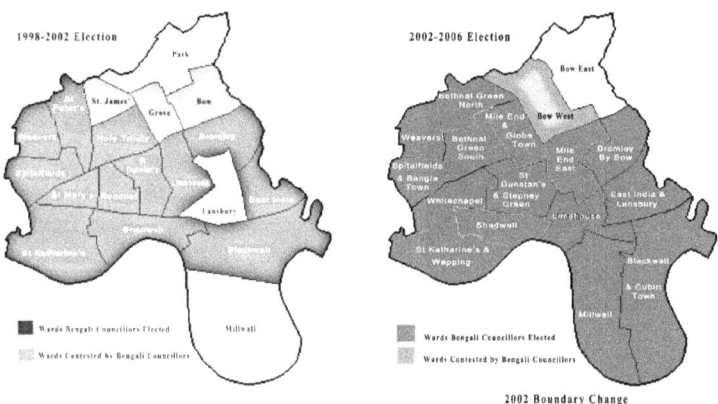

The boundary changed again in 2002, this manipulated the election results.

2006-2010 Election

2010-2014 Election

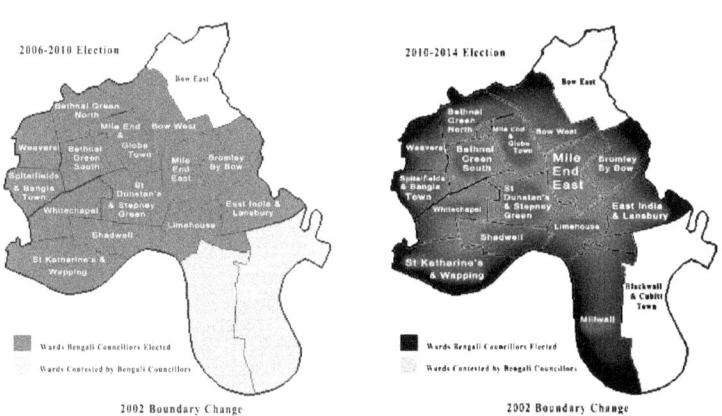

2014-2018 Election

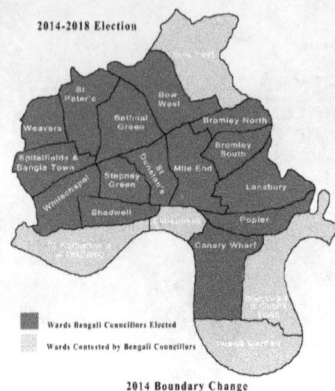

It is impressive to see the borough map as it gained more seats in the wards.

Each dark segment means that there is a Bangladeshi councillor elected.

These pictures of the map paints "literally" the map of Tower Hamlets, London, England, Great Britain, United Kingdom. The Sylheti communuty has had direct impact and influence; and the community should take reference, and not fall in to complacentcy.

The boundary changed again in 2014 to manipulate the elections and how many seats to be contested.

Full Election Results

1982-2014

In this section you have the full election result list year by year, ward by ward. This is to illustrate a picture of what they got in to and who and how many people were contesting the wards.

St Katherine's		
Year	Electorate	Turnout (%)
1982	7,235	35.3
Name	Party	Votes
Mian Md.Asik, Ali	Lab	1123
G.W. Allen	Lab	1096
J.R Ramanoop	Lab	946
M.A. Borrelli	SDP	740
Rev. D.M. Mason	SDP	722
J.R. York Williams	SDP	699
R.A. Cook	C	288
Ms L.E. Fisher	C	286
Mrs C. Cook	C	283
G. Simons	Ind Lab	198
Mrs R.E. Perkins	Ind Lab	188
Shahab U. Ahmed	Ind	185
J. Rees	Com	170
Mohammed A. Haque	Ind	65

St Mary's		
Year	Electorate	Turnout (%)
1982	4627	30.4
Name	Party	Votes
R.W. Ashkettle	Lab	877
B. Saunders	Lab	834
G.J. Palfrey-Smith	SDP	241
Rafique Ullah	SDP	205
M.S. Levitas	Com	172
R. Pearson	C	151
J.N. Razzak	C	115
Qudratul Islam	SDP WA	-

Spitalfield		
Year	Electorate	Turnout (%)
1982	4,873	35.8
Name	Party	Votes
Mohammed Nurul Huque	Ind	638
Mrs A Elboz	Lab	560
Ms S.M. Carlyle	Lab	556
Syed Nurul Islam	Ind	530
S. Corbishley	Lab	496
W. Kelly	SDP	417
Muhammed G. Mustafa	SDP	407
G.G.N. White	SDP	401
Abdul Gofur	Ind	173
Sherajul. Hoque	Ind	157

Weavers		
Year	Electorate	Turnout (%)
1982	7,221	37.4
Name	Party	Votes
J.A. Shaw	L	1496
P.J. Hughe	L	1435
K.B. Appiah	L	1396
E. Bishop	Lab	754
W. Harris	Lab	664
Ms S.A. Tyley	Lab	612
R. Dyer	C	267
Mohammed.A. Hussain	Ind	246

1986-1990 Election

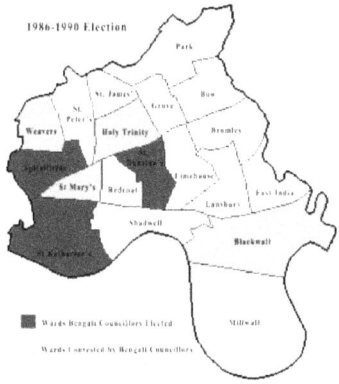

Blackwall		
Year	Electorate	Turnout (%)
1986	4,139	43.2
Name	Party	Votes
Ms C.L. Shawcroft	Lab	834
J.P. Mathew	SDP	788
Sunahwar Ali	Lab	661
R.P. Neale	SDP	657
R.G. Hughes	C	129

Holy Trinity		
1986	6,836	44.7
S.J. Charters	L	1526
Miss B.J. Knowles	L	1445
J.P. Nudds	L	1351
M.S. Chalkley	Lab	1225
G.A Cade	Lab	1167
Salim Ullah	Lab	1025
D. Ettridge	BNP	212
A.L Norton	C	138
Ms A.M. Pedlingham	C	105

St Dunstan's

Year	Electorate	Turnout (%)
1986	6,742	40.7

Name	Party	Votes
Ms S.M Carlyle	Lab	1227
T.F Sullivan	Lab	1191
Jahangir Alam	Lab	1142
J.P Brett-Freemna	L	1058
Ms L.A. Morpurgo	L	924
P.D. Truscott	L	911
R.S. Evans	NF	256
Ms M.A Bashford	C	241
K.R Collins	C	214

St Katharine's

Year	Electorate	Turnout (%)
1986	8,668	34.9

Name	Party	Votes
J.M. Rowe	Lab	1651
Ashik Ali	Lab	1562
M.S. Ahmed	Lab	1513
Konor Ali	SDP	714
G. Clark	SDP	695
Moshahid Hussain	SDP	640
A.C.George	C	461
A.M.Smith	C	410
Ms S.A. Folan	C	371
S.L. Smith	Ind	84

St Mary's

Year	Electorate	Turnout (%)
1986	4627	30.4

Name	Party	Votes
R.W. Ashkettle	Lab	948
B. Saunders	Lab	861
Abdul Barik	SDP	316
P.T. Mathurin	SDP	253
Mohammad Ali	C	218
R.J.Ingram	C	147

Spitalfields		
Year	Electorate	Turnout (%)
1986	5,648	45.2
Name	Party	Votes
Abbas Uddin Helal	Lab	1246
Gulam Mortuza	Lab	1019
P.A. Maxwell	Lab	988
Muhammed Nurul Huque	Ind	837
Akikur Rahman	SDP	590
W. Kelly	SDP	444
Syed F.Islam	Ind	402
Muhammed G. Mustafa	SDP	387
Miss J.E. Emmerson	C	215
Mrs B. Wright	Ind	199
A. Chapman	C	189

Weavers		
Year	Electorate	Turnout (%)
1986	7,505	42.5
Name	Party	Votes
J.A. Shaw	L	1645
Ms J.M. Welsh	L	1496
K.B. Appiah	L	1496
Ms S.H. Hurley	Lab	1336
Mohammed B.H. Ludi	Lab	1227
J.A.Onslow	Lab	1201
Mrs L.K.F. Ingram	C	184
Ms L.L. O'Connell	C	146

1990-1994 Election

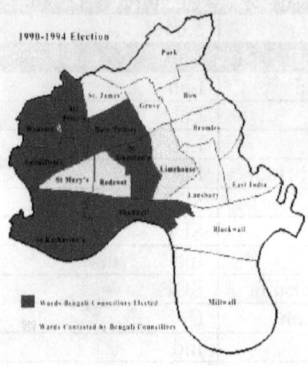

Holy Trinity (3)		
Year	Electorate	Turnout (%)
1990	6,613	49.9
Name	Party	Votes
John Nudds	L Dem	1965
Jonathon Stokes	L Dem	1909
Akikur Rahman	L Dem	1688
Edward Caunter	Lab	975
Sunahwar Ali	Lab	958
Rosemary Maher	Lab	954
Stephen Smith	BNP	290
Christine Law	G	222

Limehouse (3)		
Year	Electorate	Turnout (%)
1990	6,110	48.2
Name	Party	Votes
D.S.E. Lewis	L Dem	1655
M. Caplan	L Dem	1652
S.G. Rayment	L Dem	1625
D. Twomey	Lab	1033
Kumar Ahmed Murshid	Lab	1005
P. Seery	Lab	1004
A.B. Hopwood	GP	130

Redcoat (2)

Year	Electorate	Turnout (%)
1990	4,937	54.1
Name	**Party**	**Votes**
C.C. Birt	L Dem	1606
L.J Smith	L Dem	1558
Ashek Ali	Lab	714
C.F. Lam	Lab	647
P. Gibson	RA	106
J. Langan	RA	102
Abdul M. Khan	Ind	99
Derek W. Beackon	BNP	93
J.T. Lucy	C	51
Ms z. Peacock	C	39

St Dunstan's

Year	Electorate	Turnout (%)
1990	6,421	45.8
Name	**Party**	**Votes**
J.R Biggs	Lab	1733
D.J Gadd	Lab	1630
Shahab Uddin Ahmed	Lab	1628
T.J.B Cowley	L Dem	808
Ms C.M McNair	L Dem	751
J.S Randall	L Dem	673
D. England	GP	190
R.J Ingram	C	163
Ms S-J. Quinlan	C	138
M. Martyn	C	129

St Katherine's

Year	Electorate	Turnout (%)
1990	8,987	41.4
Name	**Party**	**Votes**
Abdul Asad	Lab	2028
Rajan Uddin Jalal	Lab	1951
Shirazul Islam	Lab	1931
R.W.J. Currie	C	850
Ms N.J. Dunsford	C	846
J. Southworth	GP	681
Abdul Hamid	C	601
Ashfaque U. Ahmed	CC	301
Muhammed Anas	CC	297

St Mary's		
Year	Electorate	Turnout (%)
1990	3632	45.6
Name	Party	Votes
R.W.Osborne	L Dem	604
Ms J.S.Ward	L Dem	596
B. Saunders	Lab	592
Ms J. Mainwaring	Lab	588
Shah M.Hoque	CC	219
E. Paris	RA	174
R.J.Warner	RA	145
Abu H.M.E. Hassain	Ind	91
Mohammed A.S. Khan	C	58
A.M. Smith	C	39

St Peter's		
Year	Electorate	Turnout (%)
1990	7,340	48.3
Name	Party	Votes
Ms B.M. Collins	L Dem	2089
Abdul Rahim	L Dem	1981
Mrs B. Wright	L Dem	1933
Fanu Miah	Lab	1232
Ms A.M. Owen	Lab	1202
T.D. Penton	Lab	1101
H. Gilbert	GP	289

Shadwell		
Year	Electorate	Turnout (%)
1990	6,241	38.1
Name	Party	Votes
A.R. Lilley	Lab	1679
J. Riley	Lab	1575
Mrs P.M. Uddin	Lab	1447
N.D. Martin	C	574
Mrs I.J.R. Taylor	C	507
T.M. Taylor	C	507

Spitalfields		
Year	Electorate	Turnout (%)
1990	5,609	42.9
Name	Party	Votes
P.A. Maxwell	Lab	1501
Gulam Mortuza	Lab	1482
Abbas Uddin (Helal)	Lab	1451
Abdul Kadir	C	372
Miss J.E. Emmerson	C	266
M. McGeorge	Ind R	248
Abdul M. Khan	CC	244
E. Reddin	GP	215
Ms J.M. Tobin	C	211
K.A. Walsh	BNP	70

Weavers		
Year	Electorate	Turnout (%)
1990	7,062	55.0
Name	Party	Votes
J.A. Shaw	L	2504
Sajjad Miah	L	2335
K.B. Appiah	L	2332
Sirajul Islam	Lab	1177
Ms J. Cove	Lab	1145
D.E. Hoyle	Lab	1121
Mohammed Abdul Rakib	Ind	77
Shundor M Ali	C	66
Shelim Uddin	C	41

1994-1998 Election

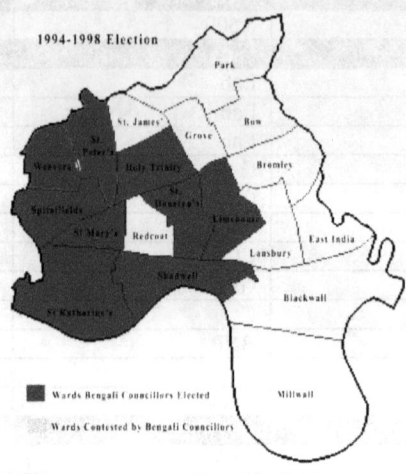

Holy Trinity		
Year	Electorate	Turnout (%)
1994	6,267	58.1
Name	Party	Votes
N. Ahmed	Lab	1407
Ms L. Gregory	Lab	1398
J. Ramanoop	Lab	1258
Ms N.K. Gale	L Dem	1039
J.S. Stokes	L Dem	1002
D.M. King	BNP	786
Mrs L. Miller	BNP	743
E. J. McHale	BNP	737
A. Rahman	L Dem	722
J.P Nudds	Ind L Dem	680
R.H. Klein	GP	165

Limehouse		
Year	Electorate	Turnout (%)
1994	5191	54.3
Name	Party	Votes
D.J. Edgar	Lab	1592
J.P. Ryan	Lab	1562
S. Alom	Lab	1559
M. Caplan	L Dem	989
Ms G. Lee	L Dem	886
S.G. Rayment	L Dem	858
P.A. Goodman	C	109
M.T Khan	Ind	98
H.C Smith	C	88
S Samih	C	71

St Dunstan's		
Year	Electorate	Turnout (%)
1994	6,421	45.8
Name	Party	Votes
J.R Biggs	Lab	2213
M.S.Uddin	Lab	1965
D.J. Gadd	Lab	1964
P.K. Wearne	L Dem	601
A.M Khan	L Dem	589
Ms L.A. Morpurgo	L Dem	552
M. Miah	Ind	239

St Katherine's		
Year	Electorate	Turnout (%)
1994	9,182	47.6
Name	Party	Votes
A. Asad	Lab	2131
Ms D. Jones	Lab	2116
R.U. Jalal	Lab	2020
D.J. Goodwin	L Dem	1195
Ms J. Harriot	L Dem	1167
A.H.S. Miah	L Dem	1127
A.H. Ali	Ind Lab	537
K.A. Bell	C	381
Ms P.A. Singleton	C	334
A.C. Thompson	C	308
J. Isaacs	Ind R	300
Ms G.R. Tilly	Ind	150

St Mary's		
Year	Electorate	Turnout (%)
1994	4,322	54.7
Name	Party	Votes
Ms A. Linton	Lab	1625
B.M. Alom	Lab	1560
R. Bowler	Ind L Dem	551
R.J. Warner	Ind L Dem	545
A. Ali	L Dem	141
M.A.S. Khan	C	104

St Peter's		
Year	Electorate	Turnout (%)
1994	8,110	52.9
Name	Party	Votes
P.A. Maxwell	Lab	2092
A. Uddin	Lab	2010
R.V. Marney	Lab	1967
Ms A.E. Ambrose	Ind L Dem	893
P. Maxwell	BNP	889
Ms K. Caulfield	Ind L Dem	876
Mrs B. Wright	Ind L Dem	803
S.S.Islam	L Dem	627
M.P.J. Patton	L Dem	567
Miss J.E. Emmerson	C	161
C.W. Southcombe	C	128

Shadwell		
Year	Electorate	Turnout (%)
1994	6,832	50.9
Name	Party	Votes
A.R. Lilley	Lab	1870
Mrs P.M. Uddin	Lab	1652
A. Shukur	Lab	1635
R.F. Roberts	L Dem	889
Ms V.L. Ocuneff	L Dem	776
H. Miah	L Dem	730
A. Miah	Ind Lab	523
P.H. Powell	C	367
P.W.E. Ingham	C	294
I.C. Dale	C	293
D.J. Baker	GP	261

Spitalfields		
Year	Electorate	Turnout (%)
1994	5,950	52.6
Name	Party	Votes
Syed A. Mizan	Lab	1937
Gulam Mortuza	Lab	1864
A. Rahman	Lab	1740
Mohammed Nurul Huque	L Dem	1018
Syed Nurul Islam	L Dem	1013
M.A. Matin	L Dem	935
U. Mohi	Ind Lab	296

1994-1998 Election

Wards Bengali Councillors Elected
Wards Contested by Bengali Councillors

Weavers		
Year	Electorate	Turnout (%)
1994	6745	52.3
Name	Party	Votes
S. Ali	Lab	1518
Ms V.L. Peters	Lab	1462
A.C Jacob	Lab	1427
J.A. Shaw	Ind L Dem	1224
T.B. Milson	Ind L Dem	1044
K.B. Appiah	L Dem	937
N. Uddin	Ind L Dem	922
S. Miah	L Dem	882

1998-2002 Election

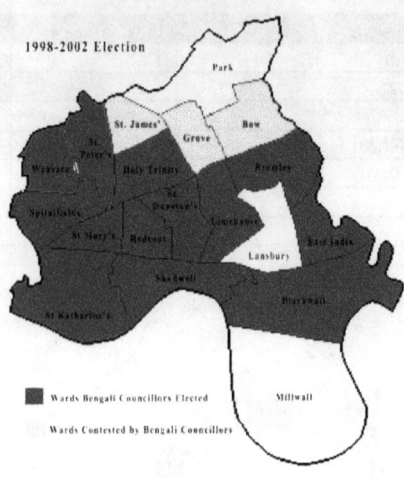

Blackwall		
Year	Electorate	Turnout (%)
1998	3,889	34.2
Name	Party	Votes
S.L Wright	Lab	701
Khan Ahmed Nuwayid Murshid (Kumar)	Lab	691
Ms J.M Jackson	L Dem	287
Ms P.A. Ramsay	L Dem	242
Hon. C.B.G. Hayhoe	C	128
Ms S. Hoile	C	107

Bromley		
Year	Electorate	Turnout (%)
1998	7.225	36.1
Name	Party	Votes
Abdul Aziz Sardar	Lab	1504
Ms C.M.Hinvest	Lab	1293
Mrs B. Chattopadhyay	Lab	1116
B. Cameron	L Dem	666
Ms R. Peters	L Dem	580
R.L. Coverson	L Dem	547
J.S. Livingstone	C	239
Ms B.J. Perrott	C	187
G.M. Price	C	157

East India		
Year	Electorate	Turnout (%)
1998	4,606	31.8
Name	Party	Votes
Brian Joseph Son	Lab	826
Rajib Ahmed	Lab	790
N.P. Huxted	L Dem	432
Ms A.J. Steggles	L Dem	647
N. Cross	C	129

Grove		
Year	Electorate	Turnout (%)
1998	4,183	42.0
Name	Party	Votes
Ms J.I. Ludlow	L Dem	874
F.C. Hunn	L Dem (Ind)	848
O.M Jacobs	Lab	704
J. Swain	Lab	647
Syed Enamul Hoque	C	113

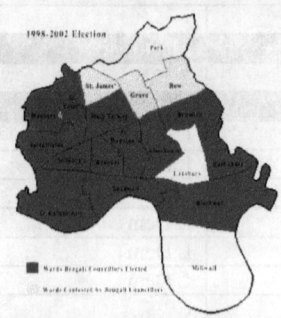

Limehouse		
Year	Electorate	Turnout (%)
1998	6175	38.5
Name	Party	Votes
Helal Uddin Abbas	Lab	928
D.J. Edgar	Lab	778
Soyful Alom	Lab	771
W.E. Wakefield	Ind	520
T.J McNally	L Dem	443
M. Caplan	Ind	441
S.G. Rayment	L Dem	431
Abu Hamid MMohammed Equbal Hossain	Ind	425
Parvin Begum	Ind	402
M.J. Pantling	L Dem	399
D. England	Ind	388
Motiur Rahman	C	260
Ms P. Drew	C	101
P.A. Goodman	C	84

Redcoat		
Year	Electorate	Turnout (%)
1998	4,639	38.3
Name	Party	Votes
Ataur Rahman	Lab	922
D.P Bayat	Lab	906
J. Langan	L Dem	636
Ms J.G. Harriott	L Dem	599
R.J.M Neill	C	129

St Dunstan's		
Year	Electorate	Turnout (%)
1998	6,224	32.7
Name	Party	Votes
J.R Biggs	Lab	1412
Shahab Uddin. Ahmed	Lab	1231
Mohammed Shahab Uddin	Lab	1220
Mrs E. Hill	C	602

St James'		
Year	Electorate	Turnout (%)
1998	5,234	40.4
Name	Party	Votes
M.E. Taylor	Lab	941
Ms L.K. Melvin	Lab	889
B.P. Martin	L Dem	847
J.D.M. Griffiths	L Dem	841
P. Maxwell	BNP	168
P.E. McHale	BNP	168
Mohammed Hashmot Ullah	C	89

St Katherine's		
Year	Electorate	Turnout (%)
1998	10689	32.1
Name	Party	Votes
Ms D. Jones	Lab	1582
Abdul Asad	Lab	1496
Anamul Hoque	Lab	1333
Miss J.E. Emmerson	C	1206
Mostofa Miah	C	1082
G.R.Glover	L Dem	610
Hilal Miah	L Dem	540
Mrs P. Snooks	L Dem	528

St Mary's		
Year	Electorate	Turnout (%)
1998	4,346	37.8
Name	Party	Votes
M. Uz-Zaman	Lab	826
A.K. Heslop	Lab/Co-op	819
Habibur Rahman Choudhury	C	358

St Peter's

Year	Electorate	Turnout (%)
1998	8,260	36.5

Name	Party	Votes
Jusna Begum	Lab	1405
Raja Miah	Lab	1223
R.V. Marney	Lab	1218
Mohammed Jainal Uddin Choudhury	L Dem	802
Ms K.E.Cook	Ind L Dem	798
B.K. Lafferty	Ind L Dem	590
Mrs B. Wright	Ind L Dem	586
T.O'Flaherty	L Dem	460
M. Elston	L Dem	441
Ms J.M. Tarby	C	237

Shadwell

Year	Electorate	Turnout (%)
1998	8014	31.3

Name	Party	Votes
M.J. Keith	Lab	1346
Bodrul Mohammed Alom	Lab	1229
Abdus Shukur	Lab	1112
Abdul Malik	Ind	757
P.H. Powell	C	589
P.W.E. Ingham	C	547
L. Aileru-Thomas	C	490

Spitalfields

Year	Electorate	Turnout (%)
1998	6,451	33.1

Name	Party	Votes
Syed Akhtaruzzaman Mizan	Lab	1454
Gulam Mortuza	Lab	1435
Ala Uddin	Lab	1316
E. Shaikh	C	621
D. Webb	C	558

Weavers

Year	Electorate	Turnout (%)
1998		

Name	Party	Votes
Mohammed Ali	Lab	1229
Kofi Bakor Appiah	Lib	776
Kathleen Caulfield	Lib	705
Christopher Gregory Creegan	Lab	985
Abdul Majid Khan	Lib	748
Jonathan Paul Mathews	Lib	738
Terry Brian Milson	Lib	770
Justine Sillman	Lib	309
Catherine Tuitt	Lab	922
Mohammed Shahab Uddin	Con	158

2002-2006 Election

2002 Boundary Change

Bethnal Green North		
Date	Electorate	Turnout (%)
2.5.2002	8289	32.26
Name	Party	Votes
Azizur Rahman Khan	L Dem	1224
John David Macleod Griffiths	L Dem	1192
James Richard Sanderson	L Dem	1097
Stephen John Beckett	Lab	878
Raja Miah	Lab	866
Diana Ruth Johnson	Lab	833
David Cox	G	233
Anna Katherine Hoad-Reddick	G	202
Sajjadur Rahman	C	196
David George Ceaser	C	185
Brajendra Nath Chaudhuri	C	167
Neil John Thompson	G	166
William Frederick Wren	BNP	162
Glyn Robbins	Ind	119

Bethnal Green South		
Date	Electorate	Turnout (%)
2.5.2002	8636	36.94
Name	Party	Votes
Sirajul Islam	Lab	1385
Akikur rahman	L Dem	1384
Salim Ullah	Lab	1331
Nurul Karim	L Dem	1309
Raymond Victor Marney	Lab	1281
Robert Waites	L Dem	1252
Shahin Ahmed	C	239
Anamul Haque	C	201
Jonathan Michael Hackett	G	190
Nicolas Alan Sellick	C	181
Peter William Howell	G	177
Gizelle Jessen Rush	G	166

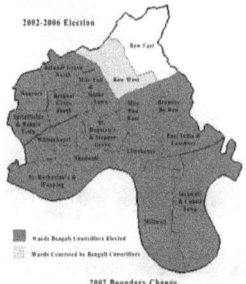

Blackwall & Cubitt Town		
Date	Electorate	Turnout (%)
2.5.2002	9081	21.48
Name	Party	Votes
Lutfur Rahman Ali	Lab	876
Julia Mainwaring	Lab	865
Anthony Julian Sharpe	Lab	793
Tim Archer	C	568
Patricia Jane Napier	C	534
Simon Paul Rouse	C	497
Barrie Alfred Blandford	L Dem	350
Alison Jane Sanderson	L Dem	310
Richard John William Ottaway	L Dem	248
Eric Pemberton	Ind	215

Bow East		
Date	Electorate	Turnout (%)
2.5.2002	7056	29.04
Name	Party	Votes
Raymond George Gipson	L Dem	1248
Nigel Edward Rupet McCollum	L Dem	1204
Marian Williams	L Dem	1155
Rupert Bawden	Lab	519
Alexander Kenneth Heslop	Lab	493
David Guppy	Lab	475
Jessica Francis Natasha Lack	G	136
Benjamin David Holt	G	125
Alastair Holmes	C	120
Susanna Gillian Webb	C	116
Volker Heineman	G	112
Timothy Hudspith	C	99

Bow West		
Date	Electorate	Turnout (%)
2.5.2002	8035	34.49
Name	Party	Votes
Janet Irene Ludlow	L Dem	1350
Hilary Susan Phelps	L Dem	1149
Martin James Rew	L Dem	1115
Ala Uddin	Lab	946
Belle Harris	Lab	939
Geoffrey Thorington-Hassel	Lab	887
Janice Dawn Cartwright	G	280
Sandra Jean McLeod	G	275
Kazi Nazmul Alam	C	255
Sheila McGregor	Ind	168
Francis Adrian Charles Simon Bown	C	155
Simon Matthew Gordan-Clark	C	153

Bromley By Bow		
Date	Electorate	Turnout (%)
2.5.2002	7407	34.10
Name	Party	Votes
David Edgar	Lab	1650
Abdul Aziz Sardar	Lab	1641
Khaled Reza Khan	Lab	1586
Brian Lawrence Abson	L Dem	353
Abdul Mannan	L Dem	320
Phyllis Doreen Sheehan	L Dem	310
Matthew Sebastian Corbishley	G	225
James McLachlan	C	204
Barbara Jean Perrott	C	186
Robert James McGillivray Neill	C	178
Hidr Yildirim	G	132

East India & Lansbury		
Date	Electorate	Turnout (%)
2.5.2002	7634	28.44
Name	Party	Votes
Ohid Ahmed	Lab	1015
Rajib Ahmed	Lab	869
Kevin Victor Morton	Lab	771
Ron Michael Harley	Lab	756
Harry Sydney Pavitt	L Dem	583
Robert Wallace	L Dem	583
Kambiz Boomla	Ind	261
Peter Golds	C	253
Gareth Llewellyn Kennedy	C	239
Gillian Thomas	C	196
Mohammed Azizul Haque	Ind	178

Limehouse		
Date	Electorate	Turnout (%)
2.5.2002	8678	26.27
Name	Party	Votes
Khan Ahmed Murshid	Lab	1026
Judith Anne Gardiner	Lab	1003
Ashton McGregor	Lab	917
Russell Peter Neale	L Dem	414
Elizabeth Emily Langley	L Dem	413
Mark Weeks	Ind	391
Philip John Briscoe	C	377
Antonio Elisa Bello	C	364
Richard Winfield	L Dem	358
Christopher David Godfrey	C	339

Mile End & Globe Town		
Date	Electorate	Turnout (%)
2.5.2002	8045	31.66
Name	Party	Votes
Mohammed Jainal Uddin Chowdhury	L Dem	1108
Rofique U Ahmed	Lab	1042
Barrie Charles Duffey	L Dem	1008
Rosina Stella Tucker	L Dem	950
Sharmin Shajahan	Lab	778
Graham Malcolm Taylor	Lab	727
Jahidul Hoque	C	326
Christopher William Coombes	G	267
Amelia Jo Gordon	G	218
Michael James Gwyne Fletcher	C	217
Mohammed Rezaul Karim	C	174
Jeremy Guy Hicks	G	156

Mile End East		
Date	Electorate	Turnout (%)
2.5.2002	7196	34.30
Name	Party	Votes
Helal Rahman	Lab	1326
Motin Uz-Zaman	Lab	1303
Abdus Salique	Lab	1254
Mohammed Sazzadur Rahman	L Dem	792
Bernard Cameron	L Dem	791
Rick Charles Wilson Mearns Pollock	L Dem	739
John Stuart Livingstone	C	242
Simon Armand-Smith	C	233
Stephen Philip Charge	C	213
Bill Wakefield	Ind	103

Millwall		
Date	Electorate	Turnout (%)
2.5.2002	9302	21.98
Name	Party	Votes
Alan Thomas Amos	Lab	1089
Betheline Chattopadhyay	Lab	986
Mumtaz Samad	Lab	970
Philip William Groves	C	446
Paul William Eric Ingham	C	422
Alison Louise Newton	C	420
Malcolm James Magregor Cuthbert	L Dem	313
Jean Stokes	L Dem	245
Ian Kevin McDonald	L Dem	241
Gordon Tom Callow	BNP	204
Susan Gibson	Ind	200

Shadwell		
Date	Electorate	Turnout (%)
2.5.2002	7872	27.46
Name	Party	Votes
Manir Uddin Ahmed	Lab	1265
Prof. Michael Keith	Lab	1188
Abdus Shukur	Lab	1076
Nanu Miah	L Dem	512
William Duncan Crossey	C	512
Richard Huw Powell	C	402
Catherine Elizabeth Buttimer	L Dem	395
Maxwell William Rumney	C	334
Gary James Marsh	L Dem	327

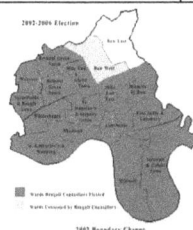

Spitalfields & Banglatown		
Date	Electorate	Turnout (%)
2.5.2002	5930	31.64
Name	Party	Votes
Helal Abbas	Lab	936
Mohammed Ghulam Mortuza	Lab	848
Lutfur Rahman	Lab	846
Md Azizur Dara Rahman	C	400
Pir Md Abdul Quium	C	345
David Webb	C	272
Ahmed Hussain	C	255
Keith Owen Magnum	G	198
Alas Uddin	L Dem	186
Muhit Ahmed	Ind	157
Annika Sander	G	146
Ismail Khubaib Malik	Ind	137
Kerry Seager	G	130
Alexander Philip Vracas	Ind	124
Sultan Ahmed	Ind	53

St Dunstan's & Stepney Green		
Date	Electorate	Turnout (%)
2.5.2002	8926	31.74
Name	Party	Votes
Ataur Rahman	Lab	1232
Nasir Uddin	Lab	1226
Mohammed Shahab Uddin	Lab	1105
Hafizur Rahman	C	828
Shamim Ahmed Choudhury	C	566
Muhammade Mominul Hoque	C	518
Paula Elizabeth Angela Palmer	L Dem	418
George Alex Crozier	L Dem	393
Mohibur Rahman	L Dem	300
Miriam Patricia Dodd	G	269
Craig Terence Williams	G	261
Frances Schwartz	G	216

St Katherine's & Wapping		
Date	Electorate	Turnout (%)
2.5.2002	8508	29.76
Name	Party	Votes
Denise Jones	Lab	1082
Shafiqul Haque	Lab	1049
Richard David Brooks	Lab	1034
Kevin Alan Noles	C	842
William Guy Darrell Norton	C	766
Toby Nevill Vintcent	C	733
Mohammed Farid Uddin Ahmed	L Dem	470
Marian Eleden	L Dem	345
Alexandra Elizabeth Sugden	LDem	318
Denis William Delderfield	Ind	259
John Divito	Ind	211

Weavers		
Date	Electorate	Turnout (%)
2.5.2002	7907	35.94
Name	Party	Votes
Abdul Matin	L Dem	1588
Louise Alexander	L Dem	1397
Tom O'Flaherty	L Dem	1288
Sirajul Islam	Lab	925
Humaiun Kobir	Lab	919
Patrick McGrogan Taylor	Lab	732
Mohammed Abdul Kadir	C	285
Benjamin Edward Hancocks	G	204
Marc Weaver	G	184
Stephen Adrian Wood	G	159
Jane Ellen Patricia Meehan	C	145
Joanne Noles	C	137
Matt Bass	Ind	51

Whitechapel		
Date	Electorate	Turnout (%)
2.5.2002	8070	33.41
Name	Party	Votes
Abdul Asad	Lab	1263
Fanu Miah	Lab	1142
Doros Ullah	Lab	1125
Mostofa Miah	C	592
Shafique Miah	C	475
Monsur Ahmed Azad	C	466
Mohammed Zaki Ahmed	Ind	462
Shamsuddin Ahmed	Ind	451
Anu Miah	Ind	407
Deborah Angela O'Flaherty	L Dem	212
Jacquiline Goodman	G	205
Brendon O'Connor	G	200
Sajaul Karim	L Dem	174
Melina La Firenze	G	167
Gulam Hussain	L Dem	162
Philip Billows	Ind	85

2006-2010 Election

2002 Boundary Change

Bethnal green North		
Date	Electorate	Turnout (%)
4.5.2006	8919	40.34
Name	Party	Votes
Muhammad Abdullah Salique	Lab	1108
Azizur Rahman Khan	L Dem	1096
Stephanie Eaton	L Dem	960
John David Macleod Griffiths	L Dem	958
Brian Robert Boag	Lab	950
Rachael Saunders	Lab	940
Abu Sufian Choudhury	Respect	882
Syed Ashraf Hussain	Respect	592
Sheila Margaret McGregor	Respect	475
Jamal Ahmed Khan	C	436
Shamsu Miah	C	413
Elaine Maureen Matby	G	398
Darren Michael Chetty	G	373
Richard John Daniel Simpson	G	345
Nishat Kabir	C	280

Bethnal Green South		
Date	Electorate	Turnout (%)
4.5.2006	9591	44.09
Name	Party	Votes
Salim Ullah	Lab	1609
Sirajul Islam	Lab	1593
Carli Harper-Penman	Lab	1436
Syeda Nurun Nahar Hussain	Respect	1342
Afzal Mahmood	Respect	1113
John William Rees	Respect	973
Akikur Rahman	L Dem	876
Mohammed Fazlul Rahman	L Dem	863
Mohammed Nanu Miah	L Dem	689
Rachel Eleanor Carless	G	327
Daniel Henry Adams	G	324
Moynul Haque Choudhury	C	264
Robert Frank Dickinson	G	253
Christopher Russell Bromby	C	237
Aurelia Diane Jane Greystoke	C	237

Blackwall & Cubitt Town		
Date	Electorate	Turnout (%)
4.5.2006	10488	32.89
Name	Party	Votes
Tim Archer	C	1317
Philip John Briscoe	C	1197
Peter Golds	C	1142
Julia Mainwaring	Lab	990
Brian Son	Lab	903
Anthony Julia Sharpe	Lab	888
Shofu Miah	L Dem	652
Abdul Kahar Choudhury	Respect	502
Barry Alfred Blandford	L Dem	463
Aysha Ali	Respect	411
Jahidul Hoque	L Dem	402
Shamsur Rahman Choudhury	Ind	362
Terence Wells	Respect	273
Eric Pemberton	Ind	152
Shelima Choudhury	Ind	75
Najma Rahman	Ind	58

Bow East		
Date	Electorate	Turnout (%)
4.5.2006	7925	37.63
Name	Party	Votes
Marc Francis	Lab	1314
Alexander Kenneth Heslop	Lab	1156
Ahmed Adam Omer	Lab	1126
Raymond George Gipson	L Dem	918
Marian Williams	L Dem	765
Andrew Paul Sage	L Dem	740
Sahra Abdi Ali	Respect	366
Andrew Ernest Palmer	C	321
Christopher Mark Nineham	Respect	309
Tansy Emily Hoskin	Respect	307
Priti Heath	C	290
William Guy Darrell Norton	C	286
Andrea Krug	G	209
Alana Jelinek	G	201

Bow West		
Date	Electorate	Turnout (%)
4.5.2006	8294	45.17
Name	Party	Votes
Anwara Ali	Lab	1483
Ann Jackson	Lab	1442
Joshua Peck	Lab	1282
Janet Irene Ludlow	L Dem	1099
Martin James Rew	L Dem	902
Stephen Clarke	L Dem	896
Anwar Hussain	C	592
Deeka Isman Adan	Respect	505
Robin David Hirsch	Respect	445
Carole Sword	Respect	425
Heather Finlay	G	415
John Foster	G	399
Frances Adrian Charles Simon Bown	C	380
Simon Matthew Gordon-Clark	C	364

Bromley By Bow		
Date	Electorate	Turnout (%)
4.5.2006	7755	48.46
Name	Party	Votes
Abdul Aziz Sardar	Lab	1689
Rania Khan	Respect	1308
Mohammed Abdul Munim	Respect	1077
Helal Rahman	Ind	1022
Jo-Anne Catherine Coles	Lab	966
Rebecca Townsend	Respect	923
David Edgar	Lab	916
Khaled Reza Khan	Ind	851
Terry McGrenera	G	342
Koyes Uzzaman Choudhury	L Dem	293
Brian Lawrence Abson	L Dem	271
Alison Louise Newton	C	271
Mohammod Jalal Uddin	L Dem	257
Barbara Jean Perrott	C	254
Kazi Nazmul Alam	C	242

East India & Lansbury		
Date	Electorate	Turnout (%)
4.5.2006	8751	39.76
Name	Party	Votes
Shiria Khatun	Lab	1461
Ohid Ahmed	Lab	1150
Rajib Ahmed	L Dem	1149
Iqbal Hossain	L Dem	944
Peter Ton-That	Lab	841
Kambiz Boomla	Respect	607
Mohammed Abdus Shahid	Respect	599
Jane Alison Archer	C	542
Ian Campbell	C	511
Paul William Eric Ingham	C	483
Caroline Spencer	L Dem	470
Martin Hetward	Respect	436
John Philips	Ind	240
Mahfuz Ahmed Khan	Ind	122

Limehouse		
Date	Electorate	Turnout (%)
4.5.2006	9352	43.01
Name	Party	Votes
Mohammed Shahid Ali	Lab	1208
Lutfa Begum	Respect	1099
Dulal Uddin	Respect	1092
Judith Anne Gardiner	Lab	1017
Ashton McGregor	Lab	960
Pennie Ann Clarke	C	933
Philip William Grove	C	886
Martin Renfred Empson	Respect	854
Kenneth Anthony Mizzi	C	847
Mohammed Aminul Haque	Ind	662
Abdul Jamal	Ind	630
Husheara Begum	L Dem	470
John Laurence Bevan	L Dem	382
Iain Chambers	L Dem	324

Mile End & Globe Town		
Date	Electorate	Turnout (%)
4.5.2006	9245	40.36
Name	Party	Votes
Rofique U Ahmed	Lab	1380
Clair Hawkins	Lab	1113
Bill Turner	Lab	1050
Mehdi Hassan	Respect	1012
Mohammed Jainal Uddin Chowdhury	L Dem	912
Kay Ballard	Respect	816
Partab Ali	L Dem	751
Glyn Robbins	Respect	717
Barrie Charles Duffey	L Dem	627
Kobir Ahmed	C	481
Gordon Thomas Callow	BNP	411
William Frederick Wren	BNP	375
Michael James Gwynne Fletcher	C	264
Andrew John McNeilis	C	223
Jeffrey Christopher Marshall	BNP	186

Mile End East		
Date	Electorate	Turnout (%)
4.5.2006	8052	41.74
Name	Party	Votes
Motin Uz-Zaman	Lab	1338
Ahmed Hussain	Respect	993
Rupert Bawden	Lab	897
Misbahur Rahman Khan	L Dem	828
Ismail Hussain	Respect	753
Jacqueline Clare Turner	Respect	752
Shamsul Islam Syed	L Dem	742
Betheline Chattopadhyay	Lab	696
Hafizur Rahman Choudhury	Ind	531
Jewel Islam	C	454
Stewart Gregory Rayment	L Dem	454
Graham Keith Collins	C	346
Caroline Jane Rouse	C	312

Millwall		
Date	Electorate	Turnout (%)
4.5.2006	11884	32.25
Name	Party	Votes
Simon Paul Rouse	C	1724
Shirley Ann Houghton	C	1685
Rupert Henry Bennett Eckhardt	C	1679
Alan Thomas Amos	Lab	1248
John Christian Cray	Lab	1128
Arip Miah	Lab	1084
Mohammed Shah Saiful Alam-Raja	Respect	606
Sybil Gertraud Cock	Respect	398
Patricia Ann Ramsey	L Dem	358
Julia Taher	Respect	312
Nigel Peter Huxted	L Dem	301
Ian Kevin McDonald	L Dem	200

Shadwell		
Date	Electorate	Turnout (%)
4.5.2006	8660	46.25
Name	Party	Votes
Shamim Ahmed Choudhury	Respect	1851
Abjol Miah	Respect	1789
Mohammed Mamun Rashid	Respect	1707
Prof. Michael Keith	Lab	1287
Humayun Kabir	Lab	1141
Abdus Shukur	Lab	1054
William Duncan Crossey	C	723
David Andrew Snowdon	C	670
Sajjadur Rahman	C	605
Catherine Elizabeth Buttimer	L Dem	266
Phyllis Doreen Sheehan	L Dem	226
Mohammed Ali	L Dem	205

Spitalfields & Banglatown		
Date	Electorate	Turnout (%)
4.5.2006	6647	43.90
Name	Party	Votes
Helal Abbas	Lab	912
Fozol Miah	Respect	866
Lutfur Rahman	Lab	860
Mohammed Ghulam Mortuza	Lab	775
Mizanur Rahman Choudhury	Ind	775
Mohammed Badrul Islam	Respect	682
Mohammed Yousuf Kamali	L Dem	548
Mohammed Abdul Mukith Choudhury	Respect	471
Dinul Hussain Shah	C	458
Mohammed Aminur Rahman	L Dem	424
Guy Jonathan Sands Burton	L Dem	354
Iqbal Hussain	C	329
Beth Jemima Sorrel Collar	G	242
Hamid Ur-Rahman Chowdury	C	241
Peter Gordon Lockley	G	191

St Dunstan's & Stepney Green		
Date	Electorate	Turnout (%)
4.5.2006	10030	44.27
Name	Party	Votes
Alibor Choudhury	Lab	1453
Abdal Ullah	Lab	1410
Oliur Rahman	Respect	1351
Mohammed Shahab Uddin	Lab	1329
Aleyk Miah	Respect	1292
Margaret Elizabeth Falshaw	Respect	954
Habibur Rahman	L Dem	747
Ataur Rahman	Ind	669
Edwin James Northover	C	630
Alexander Patrick Story	C	590
Ahmed Mustaque	L Dem	583
Farid Uddin Ahmed	L Dem	550
Jane Ellen Patricia Meehan	C	373

St Katherine's & Wapping		
Date	Electorate	Turnout (%)
4.5.2006	9222	35.46
Name	Party	Votes
Dr Emma Jones	C	1351
Shafiqul Haque	Lab	1321
Denise Jones	Lab	1290
Richard David Brooks	Lab	1231
Neil Anthony King	C	1223
Paul Michael Mawdsley	C	1153
Martine Victoria Hall	G	364
Andrew John Hall	G	359
Margaret Jia Hui Man	L Dem	349
Ron Converson	L Dem	321
Alan Robert Mead	L Dem	305

Weavers		
Date	Electorate	Turnout (%)
4.5.2006	8467	41.80
Name	Party	Votes
Abdul Matin	L Dem	1819
Louise Alexander	L Dem	1059
Tom O'Flaherty	L Dem	948
Fazlul Haque	Lab	854
Dilwara Begum	Respect	830
Amina Ali	Lab	652
Nathan David Oley	Lab	575
Paul Jason Fredericks	Respect	494
Eliza Cox	Respect	489
Catherine Elizabeth Guttman	G	364
Gias Uddin Ahmed	Ind	345
Daniel Jackson	G	321
Benjamin Edward Hancocks	G	292
Simon Marcus Ashworth Holmes	C	245
Hamida Rahman Chowdhury	C	249
Mark George Walters	C	214

Whitechapel		
Date	Electorate	Turnout (%)
4.5.2006	8467	41.80
Name	Party	Votes
Shahed Ali	Respect	1449
Abdul Asad	Lab	1107
Waiseul Islam	Respect	1084
Lutfur Rahman	Lab	1040
Doros Ullah	Lab	1019
Farhana Zaman	Respect	1004
Fanu Miah	Ind	650
Mohammed Sultan Haydar	L Dem	529
Kate Makepeace Grieve	L Dem	511
Shamsuddin Ahmed	L Dem	458
Muhammed Shafique Ahmed	C	397
Moya Margaret Ellen Frawley	C	344
Shah Md Rezaul Suhel	C	284
Mohammed Abdul Goni	Ind	186

2010-2014 Election

2002 Boundary Change

Bethnal Green North		
Date	Electorate	Turnout (%)
6.5.2010	9394	62.10
Name	Party	Votes
Zenith Rahman	Lab	1634
Giancarlo Gibbs	Lab	1586
Stephanie Eaton	L Dem	1551
Muhammad Abdullah Salique	Lab	1476
Azizur Rahman Khan	L Dem	1316
Richard Alan Macmillan	L Dem	1181
Muhammad Ansar Ali Pramanik	Respect	795
Nur Baksh	C	748
Heather Finlay	G	595
Syedun Noor	Respect	594
Nicholas Graham Lee	G	454
Alan Mak	C	445
Mathew James Smith	C	439
Samuel Peter Guttmann Hancocks	G	371
Shirin Akhter Samanta	Respect	314
Ann Edmead	Ind	156

Bethnal Green South		
Date	Electorate	Turnout (%)
6.5.2010	9821	60.29
Name	Party	Votes
Mizan Choudhury	Lab	1952
Sirajul Islam	Lab	1848
Lesley Pavitt	Lab	1519
Salim Ullah	Respect	1166
Abu Hamza Afzal Mahmood	Respect	1091
Monjur Ali	Respect	1087
Olivier Adam	L Dem	1061
Rahena Anisha	L Dem	1048
Mohammed Nasir Uddin	L Dem	779
Salina Bagum	C	520
Noor Miah	C	497
Joshua Mark Barber	G	436
Paul David Burgess	G	376
Nicolette Turki	C	367
Darren Michael Chetty	G	282

Blackwall & Cubitt Town		
Date	Electorate	Turnout (%)
6.5.2010	11885	54.86
Name	Party	Votes
Tim Archer	C	2945
Peter Golds	C	2095
Gloria Tienel	C	1945
Wais Islam	Lab	1929
Kathy Mctasney	Lab	1858
Crissy Townsend	Lab	1681
Martin Graham Carr	L Dem	1250
Graf Freda	L Dem	1097
John Griffiths	L Dem	953
Gulam Kibria Choudhury	Respect	799
Mohammed Rahman	Respect	627
Abdul Malik	Respect	577

Bow East		
Date	Electorate	Turnout (%)
6.5.2010	10432	58.63
Name	Party	Votes
Marc Francis	Lab	2297
Carli Harper-Penman	Lab	1865
Ahmed Adam Omer	Lab	1724
Dave Campbell	L Dem	1204
Rafique Ullah	L Dem	1040
Paolo Adragna	L Dem	981
Claire Louise Palmer	C	807
Phillip William Groves	C	799
Mark George Walters	C	684
Marcus Boyle	G	547
Mujibur Rahman	Respect	506
Alan Duffel	G	339
Mike Underwood	BNP	318
Joseph Charles Lucey	G	316
Ryony Shank	Respect	243
Carole Swords	Respect	223
Andrew Francis Coles	Ind	152
Emdadul Imran Haque	Ind	95
Gareth Christopher Thomas	Ind	92

Bow West		
Date	Electorate	Turnout (%)
6.5.2010	9183	65.25
Name	Party	Votes
Alan Jackson	Lab	2206
Joshua Peck	Lab	2096
Anwar Khan	Lab	2070
Sharon Bench	L Dem	1260
Anwara Ali	C	1075
Jainal Choudhury	L Dem	992
Raymond Warner	L Dem	783
Francesca Emma-louise Preece	C	723
Nicholas William Huddart	C	662
Janice Dawn Cartwright	G	576
Syed Islam	Respect	574
Aliatair James Polson	G	473
Chris Smith	G	464
Kay Ballard	Respect	356
Terry Mcgrenera	Ind	111

Bromley-By-Bow		
Date	Electorate	Turnout (%)
6.5.2010	9016	62.59
Name	Party	Votes
Khales Uddin Ahmed	Lab	2483
Rania Khan	Lab	2426
Helal Uddin	Lab	2314
Subrina Hossain	C	1105
Bodrul Islam	Respect	1100
Shamima Begum	L Dem	1055
Alkas Hoque	L em	831
Mohammed Mufti Miah	Respect	765
Kamal Uddin	Respect	737
Stuart David Hand	C	673
Koyes Uzzaman Choudhury	L Dem	653
Daryl Martin Stafford	C	599
Thomas Crosbie	G	401
Tatyana Alexandra Guttmann Hancocks	G	304

East India & Lansbury		
Date	Electorate	Turnout (%)
6.5.2010	9387	59.68
Name	Party	Votes
Ohid Ahmed	Lab	2295
Shiria Khatun	Lab	2294
Rajib Ahmed	Lab	2181
Iqbal Hossain	L Dem	1302
Martin Daniel Coxall	C	878
Kamrul Hussain	Respect	835
Zakir Hussain	Respect	820
Paul William Eric Ingham	C	810
Ahmed Mustaque	C	631
Zillur Uddin	L Dem	629
Zak Ali	L Dem	619
Asha Afi	Respect	603
Jamie Upton	G	408
James Searle	BNP	400

Limehouse		
Date	Electorate	Turnout (%)
6.5.2010	Data not present	Data not present
Name	Party	Votes
Lutfa Begum	Lab	2193
David Edgar	Lab	1880
Craig Ashton	C	1602
Graham Keith Collins	C	1525
Dulal Uddin	Respect	1500
Victoria Obaze	Lab	1488
Hafiza Islam	Respect	1357
Sakib Ershad	C	1280
Anfor Ali	Respect	1225
Hafizur Mohammed Rahman	L Dem	782
Faruk Chowdhury	L Dem	722
Jennifer Aaron-Foster	G	477
Louise Davies	G	473
Muazzam Rakol	L Dem	445
Simon Henry Earp	G	267

Mile End & Globe Town		
Date	Electorate	Turnout (%)
6.5.2010	10509	59.48
Name	Party	Votes
Rofique U Ahmed	Lab	2214
Bill Turner	Lab	2005
Amy Whitelock Gibbs	Lab	1824
Shamsul Haque	L Dem	1279
Rafique Ahmed	L Dem	1179
Syed Shikul Islam	L Dem	927
Ahad Ahmed Chowdhury	Respect	916
Muhammed Khoyrul Shaheed	C	883
Thomas Michael Lowe	C	680
Habib rahman	Respect	558
Ian Nigel Allsop	G	519
Tony Collins	Respect	439
Jesse Bryson	G	400
Russell Pick	BNP	309
Kalim James Patwa	G	284

Mile End East		
Date	Electorate	Turnout (%)
6.5.2010	8752	59.97
Name	Party	Votes
Rachael Saunders	Lab	2506
Motin Uz-Zaman	Lab	2067
Kosru Uddin	Lab	2056
Ahmed Hussain	C	1059
Mohammed Altaf Rahmani	Respect	967
Hafiz Choudhury	L Dem	944
Jamir Choudhury	Respect	907
Caroline June Kerswell	C	885
Bodrul Islam Choudhury	C	832
Altaf Hussain	L Dem	787
Fiyaz Ali	Respect	755
Kamrun Shajahan	L Dem	658

Millwall		
Date	Electorate	Turnout (%)
6.5.2010		DNA
Name	Party	Votes
Zara Davis	C	2959
David Snowdon	C	2693
Md Maium Miah	C	2519
John Christian Cray	Lab	2180
Doros Ullah	Lab	1943
Garry Wykes	Lab	1664
John Francis Denniston	L Dem	1362
Iain Kenedy Porter	L Dem	1177
George McFarlane	L Dem	1099
Shuily Begum	Respect	668
Muzibul Islam	Respect	498
Dave Anderson	BNP	358
Kevin Ovenden	Respect	277

Shadwell		
Date	Electorate	Turnout (%)
6.5.2010	9997	64.53
Name	Party	Votes
Alibor Choudhury	Lab	1915
Harun Miah	Respect	1628
Rabina Khan	Lab	1539
John Houghton	Lab	1536
Khaled Reza Khan	C	1251
Mamun Rashid Respect	Respect	1250
Nasima Begum	C	1134
Monjur Alam	Respect	807
Muhammed Nazrul Alom	L Dem	700
Jewel Choudhury	L Dem	603
Mostaque Hussain	L Dem	595

Spitalfields & Banglatown		
Date	Electorate	Turnout (%)
6.5.2010	7811	56.48
Name	Party	Votes
Lutfur Rahman	Lab	1660
Shelina Akhtar	Lab	1545
Helal Abbas	Lab	1500
Fozol Miah	Respect	1068
Ben Aric Dter	L Dem	839
Moniruzzaman Syed	L Dem	673
Philip Vracas	C	571
Sadek khan	C	561
Jewel Ahmed Toropdar	L Dem	532
Asad Ahmod	C	492
Nico Aspinall	G	483
Ahad Ali	Respect	441
Alibaba Prasad	Respect	437
Md Salim Hossain	G	265
Shah Yousuf	Ind	141

St Dunstan's & Stepney Green

	Electorate	Turnout (%)
6.5.2010	11014	62.01

Name	Party	Votes
Abdal Ullah	Lab	2376
Oliur Rahman	Lab	2319
Judith Gardiner	Lab	2078
Mahbub-Mamun Alam	Respect	1458
Abul Hussain	Respect	1261
Shahar Imran	Respect	1150
Aleyk Miah	C	1136
Ahbab Miah	L Dem	1106
Sufian Choudhury	L Dem	1038
Harun Rashid	C	995
Kaltun Omar Ali	L Dem	923
Christpher Wilford	C	849
Kirsty Chestnutt	G	595
Margaret Ann Crosbie	G	504
Frances Schwartz	G	410
Mohammed Shahab Uddin	Ind	297

St Katherine's & Wapping

Date	Electorate	Turnout (%)
6.5.2010	9429	62.52

Name	Party	Votes
Dr Emma Jones	C	1623
Shafiqul Haque	Lab	1455
Denise Jones	Lab	1447
Neil Anthony King	C	1414
Paul Michael Mawdsley	C	1383
Prof. Michael Keith	Lab	1330
Geoffrey Juden	L Dem	732
Muhammad Abdul Hye Chowdhury	Respect	491
Quadri Mamun	L Dem	454
Muhammed Shafiq Islam	Respect	453
Elvyra Sadiene	L Dem	445
Dilwara Ali	Respect	418
Martine Hall	G	395
John Foster	G	388
Alana Jelinek	G	247

Weavers		
Date	Electorate	Turnout (%)
6.5.2010	8857	62.02
Name	Party	Votes
Kabir Ahmed	Lab	2082
Anna Siobhan Lynch	Lab	1895
M. A. Mukit MBE	Lab	1532
Philip Baker	L Dem	1382
Sajjad Miah	L Dem	1179
Tim O'Flaherty	L Dem	1099
Yousuf Khan	Respect	1009
Fazlul Haque	Respect	892
Rob Hoveman	Respect	728
Akhtar Imran Ahmed	C	667
Gias Uddin Ahmed	C	640
Catherine Elizabeth Guttmann	G	628
Daniel Jackson	G	516
Ben Hancocks	G	496
Abdi Omar Hassan	C	477

Whitechapel		
Date	Electorate	Turnout (%)
6.5.2010	10663	58.30
Name	Party	Votes
Shahed Ali	Lab	2158
Aminur Khan	Lab	2091
Abdul Asad	Lab	2003
Saleh Ahmed	L Dem	1119
Lutfur Rahman	Respect	1114
Kamal Uddin Ali	L Dem	1069
Ahad Abdul	C	1044
Abdulla Almamun	Respect	1004
Fanu Mia	C	915
Shamim Rahman	L Dem	906
Saidul Alom	Respect	890
DAvid Nolan fell	C	832
Richard James Leyland	G	599
Raymond Waring	G	383
Mohammed Shahab Uddin	G	335

Each of these tables paint a picture of how their battles were fought, won and lost.

2014-2018 Election

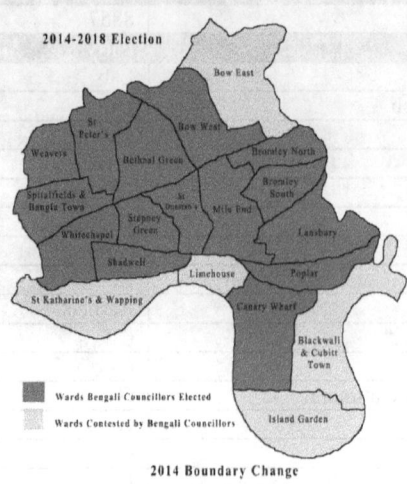

2014 Boundary Change

Bethnal Green		
Date	Electorate	Turnout (%)
22.5.2014	14085	47.63
Name	Party	Votes
Amy Whitelock Gibbs	Lab	2911
Sirajul Islam	Lab	2292
Shafiqul Haque	THF	2048
Abdirashied Gulaid	Lab	2038
Babu Choudhury	THF	1792
Salim Ullah	THF	1652
Chris Thorn	GP	1362
Kamrun Shajahan	L Dem	629
Lubov Zsikhotska	UKIP	622
Alan Mak	C	460
Meera Amrish Patel	C	330
Ellen Kenyon Peers	TUSC	327
Clive Heemskerk	TUSC	254
Taz Khalique	C	238

Blackwall & Cubit Town		
Date	Electorate	Turnout (%)
22.5.2014	9193	31.64
Name	Party	Votes
Dave Chesterton	Lab	956
Christopher James Chapman	C	877
Candida Ronald	Lab	875
Anusur Rahman	Lab	872
Gloria Rose Thienel	C	815
Geeta Mohan Kasanga	C	762
Faruk Khan	THF	744
Kabir Ahmed	THF	726
Mohammed Aktaruzzaman	THF	713
Diane Lochner	UKIP	240
Paul Shea	UKIP	190
Anthony Registe	UKIP	188
Katy Guttman	G	110
Mark Lomas	G	98
Chris Smith	G	74
Elaine Bagshaw	L Dem	71
Richard Flowers	L Dem	68
Stephen Clarke	L Dem	58
Ellen Kenyon Peers	TUSC	11
John Peers	TUSC	11
Mohammed Akhlaqur Rahman	Ind	11

2014 Boundary Change

Bow East		
Date	Electorate	Turnout (%)
22.5.2014	11244	45.86
Name	Party	Votes
Rachel Blake	Lab	2611
Marc Francis	Lab	2308
Amina Ali	Lab	2023
Sabia Kamali	THF	989
Abdus Salam	THF	977
Lucy Rees	G	935
Mickey Ambrose	THF	774
Tatyana Guttmann Hancocks	G	651
Cameron David Alexander Penny	C	520
James Thomas	C	496
Stephanie Wy Chan	C	455
Andy Spracklen	L Dem	449
Goerge Allan Paton	TUSC	221
Andy Erlam	RF AC	129

Bow West		
Date	Electorate	Turnout (%)
22.5.2014	9053	52.33
Name	Party	Votes
Joshua Peck	Lab	2439
Asma Begum	Lab	1996
Jainal Chowdhury	THF	702
Matt Smith	C	627
Anwar Ahmed Khan	Ind	619
Louise Whitmore	G	559
Alistair Polson	G	552
S. M Saiful Azam	C	441
Altaf Hussain	L Dem	328

Bromley North		
Date	Electorate	Turnout (%)
22.5.2014	6671	51.93
Name	Party	Votes
Khales Uddin Ahmed	Lab	1534
Mohammed Mufti Miah	THF	1247
Zenith Rahman	Lab	1153
Moniruzzaman Syed	THF	1046
Christopher Devlin	G	281
Aaron Wilson	G	221
Angela Carlton	C	219
Mark Peter Fletcher	C	178
Victoria Flynn	L Dem	136
Daniel McGowen	TUSC	76

Bromley South		
Date	Electorate	Turnout (%)
22.5.2014	7477	49.44
Name	Party	Votes
Helal Uddin	Lab	1565
Danny Hassell	Lab	1300
Syeda Choudhury	THF	1290
Kabir Ali	THF	1269
Ben Hancocks	G	343
Frank Richard Thienel	C	270
Srikanth Rajgopal	C	153

Canary Wharf		
Date	Electorate	Turnout (%)
22.5.2014	8327	36.53
Name	Party	Votes
Andrew George Wood	C	869
Md Maium Miah	THF	829
Debbie Simone	Lab	801
Shubo Hussain	Lab	786
Ahmed Hussain	C	782
John Cray	THF	592
Mark Adrian Webber	UKIP	327
Stephen Toal	L Dem	181
Meil Cafferky	TUSC	58

Island Gardens		
Date	Electorate	Turnout (%)
22.5.2014	9038	43.29
Name	Party	Votes
Peter Golds	C	1345
Andrew Cregan	Lab	1244
Gloria Thienel	C	1200
Raju Rahman	Lab	951
Belal Uddin	THF	648
Kathy McTasney	THF	515
Wayne Lochner	UKIP	464
Doug Oliver	L Dem	261
John Peers	TUSC	100

Limehouse		
Date	Electorate	Turnout (%)
22.5.2014	4331	48.26
Name	Party	Votes
Craig Aston	C	786
Catherine Overton	Lab	730
Mashuk Ahmed	THF	341
Matt Lomas	L Dem	105
David Hyland	UKIP	104

Lansbury		
Date	Electorate	Turnout (%)
22.5.2014	10472	51.29
Name	Party	Votes
Rajib Ahmed	Lab	2184
Shiria Khatun	Lab	1952
Ohid Ahmed	THF	1936
Dave Smith	Lab	1850
Shuily Akthar	THF	1727
Stephen John Beckett	THF	1535
Paul Shea	UKIP	732
Graham Collins	C	387
Paul William Eric Ingham	C	332
Simon McGrath	L Dem	232
Mohammed Riaz	C	228
Pete Dickenson	TUSC	190

Mile End		
Date	Electorate	Turnout (%)
22.5.2014	12049	49.58
Name	Party	Votes
Shah Alam	THF	2315
David Edgar	Lab	2268
Rachael Saunders	Lab	2139
Mohammed Shaid Ali	THF	2052
Motin Uz-Zaman	Lab	1801
Mustak Syed	THF	1796
Naomi Snowdon	C	597
Mushtak Abdullah	C	571
Andy Hallett	L Dem	500
Jewel Islam	C	446
Hafiz Choudhury	Ind	383
Arzoo Miah	TUSC	165

2014-2018 Election
Wards Bengali Councillors Elected
Wards Contested by Bengali Councillors
2014 Boundary Change

St Katherine's & Wapping		
Date	Electorate	Turnout (%)
22.5.2014	8116	46.28
Name	Party	Votes
Julia Luise Dockerill	C	1278
Denise Jones	Lab	1208
Neil Anthony King	C	1156
Robert Scott	Lab	956
Ahad Miah	THF	547
John Raphael Venpin	G	440
Stuart Madewell	THF	407
Granville Mills	UKIP	353
John Denniston	L Dem	319

St Peter's		
Date	Electorate	Turnout (%)
22.5.2014	13182	46.90
Name	Party	Votes
Abjol Miah	THF	2289
Clare Harrison	Lab	2089
Muhammed Ansar Mustaquim	THF	2088
Aktaruz Zaman	THF	1935
Carlo Gibbs	Lab	1914
Sanu Miah	Lab	1722
Paul Burgess	G	1114
David Cox	G	970
Azizur Rahman Khan	L Dem	802
Bertlyn Vernessa Springer	UKIP	453
Rachel Elizabeth Watts	C	342
Simon James Peter Fish	C	301
Leonard Rowlands	TUSC	222
Adrian Charles Thompson	C	113

2014-2018 Election

2014 Boundary Change

Stepney Green		
Date	Electorate	Turnout (%)
22.5.2014	8130	54.90
Name	Party	Votes
Alibor Choudhury	THF	2023
Oliur Rahman	THF	1965
Sabina Akhtar	Lab	1568
Victoria Obaze	Lab	954
Hilary Clarke	G	411
Nicholas McQueen	UKIP	387
Chris Wilford	C	209
Hugo Ciaran Mann	C	166
Martin Peter Donkin	L Dem	151

Weavers		
Date	Electorate	Turnout (%)
22.5.2014	8759	46.22
Name	Party	Votes
Abdul Chunu Mukit	Lab	1237
John Pierce	Lab	1223
Kabir Ahmed	THF	1214
Yousuf Khan	THF	1128
Chris Smith	G	557
Maureen	G	527
Pauline McQueen	UKIP	316
Louise Taggart	C	254
Alex Dziedzan	L Dem	202
Luke Ounsworth	C	197
Hugo Pierre	TUSC	113

Whitechapel		
Date	Electorate	Turnout (%)
22.5.2014	11337	42.37
Name	Party	Votes
Shahed Ali	THF	2139
Abdul Asad	THF	2117
Aminur Khan	THF	2088
Faruque Mahfuz Ahmed	Lab	1359
Robert Robinson	Lab	1190
Jamalur Rahman	Lab	1188
Maggie Crosbie	G	703
Richard John Holden	C	409
Dinah Glover	C	405
John David Macleod Griffins	L Dem	358
Nicholas Donald Anthony Vandyce	C	345
Andrew John McNeilis	UKIP	199
Michael Wrack	TUSC	139

Shadwell		
Date	Electorate	Turnout (%)
22.5.2014	8235	55.23
Name	Party	Votes
Rabina Khan	THF	2199
Harun Miah	THF	2192
Mamun Rashid	Lab	1462
Farhana Zaman	Lab	892
Katy Guttman	G	354
Des Ellerbeck	C	337
Daryl Martin Stafford	C	326
Monowara Begum	L Dem	144
Robert Williams	TUSC	141

Spitalfields & Banglatown		
Date	Electorate	Turnout (%)
22.5.2014	9316	43.69
Name	Party	Votes
Gulam Rabbani	THF	1955
Suluk Ahmed	THF	1743
Helal Uddin Abbas	Lab	1215
Tarik Khan	Lab	1015
Zachary Thornton	G	485
Jane Elizabeth Emmerson	C	349
David Nolan Fell	C	259
Ferdy North	L Dem	219
Jason Edward Turvey	TUSC	98

Date		Electorate	Turnout (%)
22.5.2014		8570	55.78
Name		Party	Votes
Ayas Miah		Lab	1967
Mahbub (Mamun) Alam		THF	1805
Abdal Ullah		Lab	1386
Rofique U Ahmed		THF	1369
Chris Kilby		G	484
Charles William Moncrieff Clarke		C	426
Martin Bryan		UKIP	369
Abdul Munim Choudhury		The Peace Party	254
Ben Mascall		C	254
Koyes Uzzaman Choudhury		L Dem	193

2014-2018 Election

2014 Boundary Change

Poplar			
Date		Electorate	Turnout (%)
22.5.2014		4210	49.64
Name		Party	Votes
Gulam Kibria Chowdhury		THF	910
Abdul Kahar Chowdhury		Lab	761
Anna Maria Mignano		UKIP	159
James Philip Robinson		C	146
Richard Macmillan		L Dem	41
Naomi Ruth Byron		TUSC	40

LBTH Mayoral

Tower Hamlets Mayoral		
Year	Electorate	Turnout (%)
21.10.2010	182482	25.60
Name	Party	Votes
Lutfur Rahman	Ind	23283
Helal Uddin Abbas	Lab	11254
Neil Anthony King	C	5348
John David Macleod Griffiths	LD	2800
Alan Duffel	G	2300

Tower Hamlets Mayoral		
Year	Electorate	Turnout (%)
22.5.2014	181871	47.58
Name	Party	Votes
Lutfur Rahman	Ind	37395
John Biggs	Lab	34143
Christopher Wilford	C	7173
Nicholas McQueen	UKIP	4819
Chris Smith	G	4699
Reetendra Nath Banerji	LD	1959
Hugo Pierre	TUSC	871
Reza Shoaib Choudhury	Ind	205
Md Kowaj Ali Khan	Ind	164
Hafiz Abdul Kadir	Ind	162

Mayor Lutfur Rahman was ousted and a re-election took place.

Tower Hamlets Mayoral		
Year	Electorate	Turnout (%)
11.6.2015	184563	37.73%
Name	Party	Votes
John Biggs	Lab	27255
Rabina Khan	Ind	25763
Peter Golds	C	5940
John Foster	G	2678
Elaine Bagshaw	LD	2152
Andy Erlam	RFAC	1768
Nicholas McQueen	UKIP	1669
Hafiz Abdul Kadir	Ind	316
Venessa Helen Hudson	AWP	305
Md Motiur Nanu Rahman	Ind	292

Battle for Parliament

Tower Hamlets Bethnal Green		
Year	Electorate	Turnout (%)
1997	74,146	60.3
Name	Party	Votes
Miss O.T. King	Lab	20697
K.H. Choudhury	C	9412
S.N.I. Dulu	L Dem	5361
D.M. King	BNP	3350
T.B. Milson	L	2963
S. Osman	Ind Lab	1117
S. Petter	GP	812
M. Abdullah	RP	557
A. Hamid	S Lab P	413

Tower Hamlets Bethnal Green		
Year	Electorate	Turnout (%)
2001	76,556	50.2
Name	Party	Votes
Miss O.T. King	Lab	19380
Shahangir Bakth Faruk	C	9323
Mrs J.I. Ludlow	L Dem	5946
Miss A.L. Bragga	GP	1666
M.P. Davidson	BNP	1211
D.W. Delderfield	NBP	888

Here, in these two tables you can see the race to become MP. 5 Bangladeshi men stood against Miss Oona King in 1997 and one in 2001. Here we see political muturity in 2001, where one candidate stood. Nevertheless the Bangladeshi candidate only secured similar votes in the borough. Both of the candidates were representing the Conservative Party and it be interesting how many of those votes would be from the wider Bangladeshi community after friends and family votes.

We can also note the BNP votes had fallen since 1998, from 3350 for D.M. King to 1211 M.P. Davidson in 2001.

A conservative vote in Tower Hamlets from the Bangladeshis is futile as majority of the people diehard Labour party supporters.

Tower Hamlets Bethnal Green & Bow		
Year	Electorate	Turnout (%)
2005	82,599	53.3
Name	Party	Votes
G. Galloway	RU	15801
Miss O.T. King	Lab	14978
S. Bahkt Faruk	C	6244
Syed Nurul Islam Dulu	L Dem	4928
J.P.W Foster	GP	1950
E. Etefia	Ind	68
Miss C. Pugh	CL	38

Tower Hamlets, Poplar & Limehouse		
Year	Electorate	Turnout (%)
2005	85,136	45.8
Name	Party	Votes
J. Fitzpatrick	Lab	15628
T.J Archer	C	8499
Oliur. Rahman	Res	6573
Mrs J.I Ludlow	L Dem	5420
T McGrenera	GP	955
Mohammed Aminul Hoque	Ind	815
T Smith	Ind	650
S.A Ademolake	Ind	470

Tower Hamlets Bethnal Green & Bow		
Year	Electorate	Turnout (%)
2010	81,243	63.25
Name	Party	Votes
Rushanara Ali	Lab	21,784
Ajmal Masroor	L Dem	10210
Abjol Miah	Res	8532
Zakir Hussain Khan	C	7071
Jeffrey Christpher Marshall	BNP	1405
Farid Bakth	G	856
Patrick Brooks	Ind	277
Alexander Rene Van-Terheyden	Ind	213
Hasib Hikmat	Ind	209
Mahmood Choudhury	Ind	100
Ahmed Abdul Malik	Ind	71

Tower Hamlets Poplar & Limehouse

Year	Electorate	Turnout (%)
2010	74,955	62.98
Name	**Party**	**Votes**
Jim Fitzpatrick	Lab	18679
Tim Archer	C	12649
Jonathon Harold	LD	8160
George Galloway	Res	5209
Wayne Lochner	UKIP	565
Andrew Osborn	Ind	470
Chris Smith	G	449
Kabir Mahmud	Ind	293
Md Aminul Hoque	Ind	167
Jim Thornton	Ind	59

Tower Hamlets Bethnal Green & Bow

Year	Electorate	Turnout (%)
2015	82727	64.29
Name	**Party**	**Votes**
Rushanara Ali	Lab	32387
Matt Smith	C	8070
Alistair Polson	G	4906
Pauline McQueen	UKIP	3219
Teena Lashmore	LD	2395
Glyn Robbins	LU - TUS	949
M Rowshan Ali	CUP	356
Jonathan Dewey	CSA	303
Alasdair Iain Henderson	WPC	203
Elliot Ball	T30-50 C	78
Jason Andrew Pavlou	RFAC	58

Tower Hamlets Poplar & Limehouse

Year	Electorate	Turnout (%)
2015	82081	62.44
Name	**Party**	**Votes**
Jim Fitzpatrick	Lab	29886
Chris Wilford	C	12962
Nicholas McQueen	UKIP	3128
Maureen Childs	G	2463
Elaine Bagshaw	LD	2149
Hugo Pierre	TUSC	367
Rene Claudel Mugenzi	RFAC	89

Abbreviations

Abbreviation	Party
BNP	British National Party
C	Conservative
CC	Tower Hamlets Community Campaign
Com	Communist Party of Great Britain
CSA	Canabis is Safer than Alcohol
CUP	Communities United Party
ELPA	East London Peoples' Alliance
GP	Green Party
II	Island Independent
ILP	Independent Labour Party
Ind	Independent (indicates an unofficial candidate when placed before a party abbreviation)
Ind R	Independent Resident
L	Liberal Party
L Dem	Liberal Democrats
Lab	Labour Party
Lab/Co-op	Labour Party and Co-operative Party joint candidate
LU-TUS	Left Unity - Trade Unionist and Socialists
M Lab	Militant Labour
NF	National Front
NLP	Natural Law Party
RA	Residents Association
RES	Respect Party
RFAC	Red-Anti-Corruption
SDP	Social Democratic Party
SU	Socialist Unity
SWP	Socialist Workers Party
T3-5C	The 30-50 Coalition
TA	Tenants Association
THF	Tower Hamlets First
TPP	The People's Party
TUSC	Trade Union Solidarity Congress
UM	Union Movement
UP	Unionist Party
WPA	Whig Party Candidate
WRP	Workers' Revolutionary Party

Bibliography

Ahmed, Faruque (2013)Bengali Politics in Britain Logic, Dynamics and Disharmony, Creation, New York, p243

Glynn, Sarah, (2017) Class, Ethnicity and Religion in the Bengali East End, A political history, Manchester University Press, UK p109, p148

Aziz, Suhail (2020) Breakthrough Memoir of a British-Trained Bangladeshi, The Book Guild Ltd, UK, p185,186

Akash, Mayar (2017) Tower Hamlets Bangladeshi Politician' Reference Book 1982-2018, Bangladeshi East End, MAPublisher, London, p105

Muhammad Anwar & Pnina Werbner (1991) Black & Ethnic Leadership in Britain, The cultural dimensions of political action, Routledge, London, p62, p63

Interviews & Discussions

Rajon Uddin Jolal –	Home visit, Telephone
Md Nurul Huque –	Home visit
Jainal Choudhury –	Telephone and Text
Akikur Rahman –	Telephone
Abdul Mukit Chunu MBE –	Home Visit, Meeting & Telephone
Helal Uddin Abbas –	Meeting
Syed Mizan –	Telephone
Phil Maxwell –	Telephone
Hugo Pierre –	Telephone
Baroness Uddin -	Text/Phone
Sunawhar Ali	Telephone, Text
Shahid Ali	Telephone
Ayas Miah	Telephone

References

1. http://www.election.demon.co.uk/[18.1.19]
2. https://democracy.towerhamlets.gov.uk[18.1.19]
3. Bengal Politics in Britain By Faruque Ahmed
4. https://books.google.co.uk/books?id=TCxKAgAAQBAJ&pg=PA216&dq=bricklane+to+bari&hl=en&sa=X&ved=0ahUKEwinoYqag7nTAhVLZ1AKHc8KC78Q6AEIUTAI#v=onepage&q=bricklane%20to%20bari&f=false
5. East London Advertiser
6. East End Life
7. Bancroft Archive Library
8. https://en.wikipedia.org/wiki/Tower_Hamlets_London_Borough_Council_election,_1986
9. https://en.wikipedia.org/wiki/Tower_Hamlets_London_Borough_Council_election,_1990[18.1.19]
10. https://en.wikipedia.org/wiki/Tower_Hamlets_London_Borough_Council_election,_1994
11. https://en.wikipedia.org/wiki/Tower_Hamlets_London_Borough_Council_election,_1998
12. https://en.wikipedia.org/wiki/Tower_Hamlets_London_Borough_Council_election,_2002
13. http://lovewapping.org/2017/01/lutfur-rahman-makes-comeback-with-new-political-party-tower-hamlets-together/[5.7.19]
14. https://www.electoralcommission.org.uk/i-am-a/party-or-campaigner/guidance-for-political-parties/pending-registration-applications/current-applications [5.7.9]
15. https://books.google.co.uk/books?id=je-IAgAAQBAJ&pg=PA63&lpg=PA63&dq=1982+nurul+huque+councillor&source=bl&ots=OBr2bpIAWl&sig=ACfU3U2hAJr6LK6MVZ0LUzjIEp4jNovTUA&hl=en&sa=X&ved=2ahUKEwjvitrm9Z_3AhWMXsAKHTaMDaAQ6AF6BAgDEAM#v=onepage&q=1982%20nurul%20huque%20councillor&f=false[19.4.22]
16. https://www.towerhamlets.gov.uk/Documents/Leisure-and-culture/Events/Altab_Ali_The_Fight_for_Equality.pdf [19.4.2022]

MAPublisher Catalogue

ISBN/Titles /Image/Author	ISBN/Titles /Image/Author	ISBN/Titles /Image/Author	ISBN/Titles /Image/Author
978-1-910499-00-9 Father to child By Mayar Akash	978-1-910499-08-5 HSJ Lakri Tura By Mayar Akash	978-1-910499-26-9 Colouring 1-10 By MAPublisher	978-1-910499-18-4 Basic Numbers 1-10 By MAPublisher
978-1-910499-16-0 River of Life By Mayar Akash	978-1-910499-09-2 HSJ Gilaf Procession By Mayar Akash	978-1-910499-27-6 Activity Numbers 1-10 By MAPublisher	978-1-910499-19-1 Number 1-100 By MAPublisher
978-1-910499-39-9 Eyewithin By Mayar Akash	978-1-910499-03-0 HSJ Mazar Sharif By Mayar Akash	978-1-910499-28-3 Activity Colouring Alphabets By MAPublisher	978-1-910499-20-7 Vowels By MAPublisher
978-1-910499-32-0 WG Survivor By Mayar Akash	978-1-910499-06-1 Hazrat Shahjalal By Mayar Akash	978-1-910499-68-9 The Adventures of Sylheti mazars By Mayar Akash	978-1-910499-21-4 Alphabet Consonants By MAPublisher
978-1-910499-66-5 Yesteryears By Mayar Akash	978-1-910499-07-8 HSJ Urus By Mayar Akash	978-1-910499-38-2 Bite Size Islam: 99 Names of Allah By Mayar Akash	978-1-910499-22-1 Vowels & Short By MAPublisher

ISBN/Titles /Image/Author	ISBN/Titles /Image/Author	ISBN/Titles /Image/Author	ISBN/Titles /Image/Author
978-1-910499-15-3 Anthology One By Penny Authors	978-1-910499-36-8 Delirious By Liam Newton	978-1-910499-52-8 Lit From Within By Ruth Lewarne	978-1-910499-57-3 The Vampire of the Resistance By Ruth Lewarne
978-1-910499-17-7 Anthology Two By Penny Authors	978-1-910499-54-2 Book of Lived v6 Penny Authors	978-1-910499-49-8 Cry for Help By B. M. Gandhi	978-1-910499-55-9 Riversolde By Meriyon
978-1-910499-29-0 Book of Lived v3 By Penny Authors	978-1-910499-37-5 When You Look Back By Rashma Mehta	978-1-910499-14-6 The Halloweeen Poem by Zainab Khan	978-1-910499-70-2 Smiley & The Acorn By Roger Underwood
978-1-910499-351 V4 Book of Lived By Penny Authors	978-1-910499-37-5 My Dream World By Rashma Mehta	978-1-910499-69-6 Consciousness By Mustak Mustafa	978-1-910499-40-5 World's First University By Giasuddin Ahmed
978-1-910499-50-4 Book of Lived v5 By Penny Authors	978-1-910499-53-5 Angel Eyez By Rashma Mehta	978-1-910499-73-3 Book of Lived v7 By Penny Authors	978-1-910499-56-6 The Warrior Queen By Giasuddin Ahmed

All books are available on-line, Google the titles and they will take you to the sites where you can acquire copies.
https://www.waterstones.com/author/mayar-akash/1973183 [3.11.21]

ISBN/Titles /Image/Author	ISBN/Titles /Image/Author	ISBN/Titles /Image/Author	ISBN/Titles /Image/Author
978-1-910499-58-0 EEP:Tower Hamlets, Random, One Mayar Akash	978-1-910499-60-3 EEP:Tower Hamlets, Random, Two By Mayar Akash	978-1-910499-05-4 Tide of Change By Mayar Akash	978-1-910499-51-1 Brick & Mortar By Mayar Akash
978-1-910499-61-0 Grenfell Tower By Mayar Akash	978-1-910499-63-4 EEP: Power Houses, Clove Crescent By Mayar Akash	978-1-910499-71-9 Altab Ali Murder By Mayar Akash	978-1-910499-31-3 Pathfinders By Mayar Akash
978-1-910499-62-7 EEP: Community Service 1992-1993 By Mayar Akash	978-1-910499-64-1 EEP:Bancroft Estate By Mayar Akash	978-1-910499-11-5 Re-Awakening By Mayar Akash	978-1-910499-13-9 Chronicle of Sylhetis of UK By Mayar Akash
978-1-910499-59-7 EEP:Brick Lane, Spitalfields By Mayar Akash	978-1-910499-72-6 25th Anniversary of Bangladesh By Mayar Akash	978-1-910499-12-2 Young Voice Mayar Akash	978-1-910499-42-9 Bangladeshi Fishes By Mayar Akash
978-1-910499-65-8 PYO Polish Exchange 1992 By Mayar Akash	978-1-910499-30-6 TH Bangladeshi Politicians By Mayar Akash	978-1-910499-10-8 Vigil Subotaged By Mayar Akash	978-1-910499-67-2 F. Ahmed and History By Mukid Choudhury

All books are available on-line, Google the titles and they will take you to the sites where you can acquire copies.

ISBN/Titles /Image/Author	ISBN/Titles /Image/Author	ISBN/Titles /Image/Author	ISBN/Titles /Image/Author
978-1-910499-43-6 My Life Book 1 By Mayar Akash	978-1-910499-44-3 My Life Book 2 By Mayar Akash	978-1-910499-45-0 My Life Book 3 By Mayar Akash	978-1-910499-46-7 My Life Book 4 By Mayar Akash
978-1-910499-47-4 My Life Book 5 By Mayar Akash	978-1-910499-75-7 Bangladeshis in Manchester - Oral History, Part 1 By M.A. Mustak	978-1-910499-74-0 Peter Fox Artist By Peter Fox	978-1-910499-78-8 On The Seventh Day By Cosette Ratliff

https://www.lulu.com/spotlight/mayarakash3bb00494 [10.11.21]

All books are available on-line, Google the titles and they will take you to the sites where you can acquire copies.